BRIGHT NOTES

THE ORDEAL OF RICHARD FEVEREL BY GEORGE MEREDITH

Intelligent Education

Nashville, Tennessee

BRIGHT NOTES: The Ordeal of Richard Feverel
www.BrightNotes.com

No part of this publication may be used or reproduced in any manner whatsoever without written permission, except in the case of brief quotations in critical articles and reviews. For permissions, contact Influence Publishers http://www.influencepublishers.com.

ISBN: 978-1-645421-66-5 (Paperback)
ISBN: 978-1-645421-67-2 (eBook)

Published in accordance with the U.S. Copyright Office Orphan Works and Mass Digitization report of the register of copyrights, June 2015.

Originally published by Monarch Press.
Ralph A. Ranald, 1966
2019 Edition published by Influence Publishers.

Interior design by Lapiz Digital Services. Cover Design by Thinkpen Designs.

Printed in the United States of America.

Library of Congress Cataloging-in-Publication Data forthcoming.
Names: Intelligent Education
Title: BRIGHT NOTES: The Ordeal of Richard Feverel
Subject: STU004000 STUDY AIDS / Book Notes

CONTENTS

1)	Introduction to George Meredith	1
2)	Introduction to George Meredith: The Relation of Meredith's Fiction to his Ideas	12
3)	Introduction to The Ordeal of Richard Feverel	50
4)	Textual Analysis	
	Chapters 1–10	61
	Chapter 11–20	81
	Chapter 21–30	98
	Chapters 31–40	112
	Chapters 41–49	126
5)	Character Analyses	140
6)	An Essay On The Relation Of Meredith's Poetry To His Fiction	148
7)	Critical Commentary	192
8)	Essay Questions and Answers	195
9)	Bibliography	202

INTRODUCTION TO GEORGE MEREDITH

Meredith was, during his lifetime, very reticent about his origins and family, and this is understandable, given his particular outlook and orientation. He actually portrayed his hidden biography in his works, especially in *The Ordeal of Richard Feverel*, in *Evan Harrington*, and in the great sequence of fifty sonnet-like poems, *Modern Love*. The first and third of these, discussed at some length in the light of the biographical data now available to us, deal with Meredith's frightfully unhappy marriage to Mary Ellen Peacock. The second, the most autobiographical of all, deals with Meredith's childhood and with his family background.

SOCIAL BACKGROUND

Meredith, who became the chronicler of the English Country Establishment - the half-million (at most) favored people who were members of landed gentry and agricultural upper-class or upper-middle-class families, and who lived on comfortable country estates in nineteenth-century England with incomes derived from inheritances, from agriculture, from rents - indeed, from anything other than manufacturing or trade - was by no means of this class himself. This is the first fact to be noted in his biography. He was not, in the cheap sense, a social snob; rather, he valued certain traits and qualities in the English aristocracy and landed gentry so highly that he attributed to some, but by no means all, of this group the very highest qualities of human perfection. The aristocracy came to stand for the best in all men; the highest development of the race. Now, there is much to be said against the Meredithian outlook, but before one can criticize - if criticism is indeed indicated - one must understand what Meredith was saying in his sometimes aphoristic and obscure poetic language. And to understand what he was saying, one must understand him, to whatever degree it is possible.

George Meredith was born at Portsmouth, the English naval port, on February 12, 1828; he claimed later royal Welsh ancestry, but the truth was that both his father, Augustus Armstrong Meredith, born in 1797, and his grandfather, Melchisedek Meredith, were tailors. His grandfather built up an excellent business in Portsmouth during the Napoleonic Wars as a naval outfitter, tailoring uniforms for naval officers. Unfortunately, however, the business fell off because of the advent of peace in 1815, and also because Augustus was never much of a tailor or businessman; so George simply did not have a wealthy or even a comfortably well-off upbringing. He was a tailor's son, and an unsuccessful tailor's at that. Although this is certainly no crime, a consideration which may simply not occur to many readers of Meredith's works is that there were two trades or occupations in the England of the nineteenth and earlier centuries which had somehow become invested with a peculiar contempt on the part of society; that of the tinker, and that of the tailor.

Why this contempt should be present is complicated; perhaps the tinker, as a repairer of damaged pots and pans, was likely to be an itinerant workman, with the hint of something disreputable about him. The case of the tailor is even more complicated. A tailor is a "tradesman" of relatively low status in the England of the period; perhaps it may hinge on nothing more than the reputation of tailors for being underpaid and exploited. One can read documents of both Thomas Carlyle and Charles Kingsley, Meredith's literary contemporaries, to see some horrific doings in the clothing sweatshops of London. At any rate, Meredith did his best during his lifetime to conceal his actual origins, knowing instinctively that the classes he worshipped from afar - or near - would never be able to bring themselves to accept him if the simple two-word phrase: "tailor's son" were whispered.

In one of the books about Meredith published during his lifetime, E. J. Bailey's *The Novels of George Meredith* (London, 1908: Unwin), appears this interesting passage, at the beginning of Chapter Two:

> **"The first decade of Meredith's literary career was the third of his life-time. Born in Hampshire, February 12, 1828, he lost during his childhood his Welsh father and Irish mother, and thereupon becoming a ward in chancery was sent to Germany for his education."**

The only trouble with this passage is that at least two important facts in it are purely figments of someone's imagination, whether Meredith's or Mr. Bailey's, but ultimately probably the former. The truth is that Meredith's father, while he became estranged from his son in the same manner, without the dramatic circumstances, as did Sir Austin Feverel become estranged from Richard, lived for a number of years after George was grown, and having married again, eventually left England for Cape Town.

There was some small inheritance which Meredith received from his mother, who died when he was five; it was not over a thousand pounds, which of course was more than the majority of the population ever saw then, but was in no way a fortune. And this money was tied up in trust for George, with his father unable to touch it, especially as his father had gone into bankruptcy in the tailoring establishment in Portsmouth when George was ten - this was in 1838. Soon thereafter, the Meredith family had moved to London, where Augustus Meredith became a journeyman-tailor in someone else's tailoring shop, a comedown for one who had had his own business and who was the son of a successful proprietor.

SCHOOLING

Meredith was sent to a rather atypical school - atypical, that is, of the class pretensions which seemed already to be his. During 1842–44, he attended a school at the German town of Neuwied, on the Rhine River between Bonn and Coblentz - and this school, among the fantastically scenic and historic surroundings, with visions of Seigfried's *Rhine Journey*, was to have a permanent effect on Meredith's thought and personality. Nature along the Rhine is, and more surely was, impressive, and some of this rather wild and lofty scenery would be with Meredith for the rest of his life, as evidenced from his unique descriptions of nature in such novels as *The Ordeal of Richard Feverel*. As poet and novelist, he could portray both the gentle and the stern aspects of nature, and at Neuwied the latter predominated. But the education he received was in advance of what he might have acquired at an equivalent school in England, for the Moravian Brothers developed in their students a general tolerance and detachment, and, what is more, there is no evidence that there was at that school the kind of corporal punishment which Meredith would undoubtedly have undergone at an English Public School of the time. The Moravian, or Bohemian, Brethren, were a Reforming Protestant Christian sect which, originally established in 1467 in what is now Czechoslovakia, may have had a considerable influence on Meredith's thought, not theologically, because after a time he dropped most belief in orthodox Christian theology, but rather in his view that some considerable reforms were necessary in the manner of living a life - if that life was to be at all satisfactory in terms of both the individual's well-being and in the progress of the human race on the evolutionary scale or ladder.

INFLUENCES

Meredith also, during this two year educational sojourn in Germany, came to know something of German philosophy and the German literary romantic movement - as did Carlyle earlier. Returning from Germany, where the noble self-abnegation and philosophy of service to one's fellow-man of Goethe had influenced him in a fundamental way, which he was to embody in his writing later, he became apprenticed to a lawyer. The young man, George Meredith, now eighteen, was destined for the profession of the Law upon his return from Germany and, in February 1846, was articled (apprenticed, without pay but with the chance to learn) to a solicitor, one Mr. Charnock, in London. Charnock himself was a young man, not more than thirty, and he seems to have been more interested in literature than in applying himself to his profession. Charnock had a far-reaching influence on Meredith's life and work, all out of proportion to his own abilities as a man of letters (apparently slight). For the lawyer introduced his articled clerk to the son of the well-known English satirist and novelist, Thomas Love Peacock.

Peacock (1785–1866) had been very friendly with Shelley before the death of that great poet in 1822; he wrote witty novels with very little plot, fantastic and poetic dialogue, and a satiric tone. The *Misfortunes of Elphin* (1829) is a fair representative of his work. Peacock, as was Shelley, was most interested in Zoroastrianism, in the eternal warfare between the principle of light, Ormuzd, and that of darkness, Ahriman, the evil deity - and it will be noted that *The Ordeal of Richard Feverel* is simply filled with expressed or implied Zoroastrian references, explained in the Commentary below. Meredith, in other words, got his Zoroastrianism, at least as a **metaphor**, from Peacock. Edward Peacock, the novelist's son, became friendly with Meredith, and introduced him not only to his father, but also to his widowed sister, Mary Ellen Peacock Nicolls. Mrs. Nicolls was nine years older than Meredith, and the mother of a three-year-old daughter at the time of their meeting; she had lost her husband, a lieutenant in the Royal Navy, rather tragically. And she became interested in the exuberant Meredith and he in her, disregarding the difference in age and the more considerable difference in temperament; they were married on August 9, 1849, after Meredith's father and stepmother had left England for Cape Town, South Africa, to make a new start there. Meredith was now legally of age, twenty-one; he had a wife, a stepdaughter, and an inheritance of a thousand pounds from his mother, an amount which was quickly spent on the support of the family. But Meredith had begun his writing career; he published *Poems*, in 1851, and two rather ephemeral prose fantasies, *The Shaving of Shagpat* (1855), and Farina (1857).

FAMILY LIFE

The difficulty was that Meredith was financially as unsuccessful at this point as his father had been. He and his wife moved in with Peacock, who did not appreciate this gesture as they were living on his bounty. The couple, both highly intelligent and emotional, quarreled bitterly, and ultimately, in 1858, Meredith's wife eloped to Italy with an artist named Wallis, who seems to have been the original of Denzil Somers in *The Ordeal of Richard Feverel* and to have evinced the same lack of personal force as Somers. Meredith was left with a young son, while Mrs. Meredith went to Capri with Wallis. A year later, she was to return to England, deserted by her lover and with a child which was not her husband's. Meredith, evidently, out of his injured pride, behaved with exceptional severity toward her. He refused to let her visit him or even see their son, until just before her premature death in 1861.

In his behavior towards his wife, Meredith showed himself to be hard and vindictive. But the event left such scars that he was to write about it twice, converting torment into art, first in *The Ordeal of Richard Feverel*, and subsequently in *Modern Love*. We have discussed in great detail this symbolic re-living and re-examination of his disastrous marriage by Meredith in these works, in the critical essays below, but it should be noted that this was the central fact of Meredith's earlier life and career, and that it led directly to *The Ordeal of Richard Feverel*.

Meredith wrote that novel during the year after his wife and her lover had gone. Both the stylistic innovations and the philosophy, as well as the plot and situation and the aphoristic method of commentary upon character, may be accounted for by Meredith's background, his associations (especially with Thomas Love Peacock), and his desire to write something which should be at once a tragicomedy and a tragedy of young love crushed by worldly values and considerations. It is worthy of note that Meredith, who wrote the novel at top speed to establish himself as a writer and to win fame and wealth, as well as to "write out" and therefore destroy the tremendous feeling of suppressed guilt over his conduct toward his estranged wife, which may have been affecting him at the time, revised the novel in 1878, or in the period of his maturity, some twenty years after the writing of *The Ordeal of Richard Feverel*. In the revision, many of the anti-feminist remarks made by Meredith earlier were toned down or eliminated, and the account of the System was changed. In general, the revision, representing second thoughts on Meredith's part about a number of matters, is much less successful or moving than was the original novel.

LITERARY CAREER

Meredith's literary career progressed after 1859 to the point where, by his death a half-century later, he was regarded as one of the greatest English novelists and poets of his age. He was never very widely read; Dickens, for example, certainly had a much wider following, as did Trollope. Meredith's style was too elliptical, his philosophy too profoundly accepting of the newly - discovered hardness and impersonality of nature, his **satire** too sophisticated and aristocratic, to win general acceptance - though in his treatment of romantic love and his idealization of women he was closer to the main line of the Victorian tradition than many realize today. While he had to proceed by indirection, he was still more frank and honest in most things, including his acceptance of the findings of nineteenth-century science, than many of his contemporaries. Only in his treatment of his personal life was he understandably quite vague and reticent, personally. In his writing, that was another story. Everything is there: his grandfather, his father, his first wife and her lover, his three sisters, who all married well and into social stations much beyond their own by birth. Lionel Stevenson's relatively recent book, *The Ordeal of George Meredith*, is an important study which helps to show the relationship between Meredith's earlier life and his work, and while in some ways it is not definitive, it is still more useful than such earlier works on Meredith as the one by Bailey cited above, which is simply inaccurate.

Meredith published *Evan Harrington* in 1860 - the most autobiographical of all his novels, even more so than *Richard Feverel*. His poetry is described separately in the general essay on the relationship of his poetry to his fiction, below, and the dates of the various collections and volumes of poetry are given. In 1864, Meredith's life turned a kind of spiritual corner, for after his second marriage, to Marie Vulliamy, he underwent a change in outlook reflected in his fiction, though to attribute this change solely to his personal happiness, which was greatly increased by this marriage, as happy as the first had been unhappy, would be naive and simplistic. Meredith was a poet and an artist, and his art could never be totally determined by his experiences.

Sandra Belloni, his third important novel, appeared in 1864. *Rhoda Fleming* came in the next year, and Vittoria, a sequel to *Sandra Belloni*, in 1866, dealt with the Italian revolutionary uprising in 1848 against the Austrians. Meredith, incidentally, had strong political interests, and covered the Austro-Italian war of 1866 as a war correspondent for the *Morning Post*, and later was an editor and staff writer on political as well as literary subjects for several magazines and newspapers.

The Adventures of Harry Richmond was published in 1871, and in the story of a father told by his son one can see the burning **theme** of family and descent still operating in Meredith's mind. Beauchamp's Career appeared in 1875, and in this novel the political interest is strong. While Meredith's interests seemed to be turning more to society in mass and to the seats of political power, as is also evidenced by one of his very strongest novels, *Diana of The Crossways* (1885), his style was becoming even more involuted, except in *Diana*. Between 1875 and 1885 Meredith also published the excellent, even brilliant, lecture on *The Idea of Comedy* and the *Uses of the Comic Spirit*, very much worth consulting for an account of Meredith's philosophy of literature and of **satire**. He also published *The Egoist* (1879), another of his very strong works, and *The Tragic Comedians* (1880), a romantic and political novel with a strong biographical thread - the biography of the Socialist politician, *Ferdinand Lassalle* (1825–64), who was a German precursor of theoretical socialism; what seems to have interested Meredith about Lassalle was his love affair with the aristocratic Helene von Donniges, whose father refused them his permission to marry and forced her to marry another, because Lassalle was not only of a lower social class than Helene, but was also Jewish. Meredith identified closely with Lassalle. The latter's death is historical; he was killed in a duel by the man, Count Racowitza, who was to become Helene's husband - killed reluctantly and pointlessly, which presents this history in the same light as the fantastic and tragic deaths of Lucy Feverel and of Harry Beauchamp.

LATER PERIOD

After 1885, it cannot be said that Meredith wrote any more first-rate novels. He published much poetry after this period, discussed below, and the novels *One of our Conquerors* (1891), *Lord Ormont and his Aminta*, *The Amazing Marriage* (1894 and 1895, respectively), and the fragmentary *Celt and Saxon*, published posthumously (1911), two years after his death. But in these four works, he seems largely to have been repeating himself.

In his total literary output, Meredith was rather uneven in quality, but at his best he did attain greatness. Like his equally great contemporary, Hardy, he was honored and decorated by the English government and people; in 1892 he was elected President of the Society of Authors, succeeding no less a writer than Tennyson; in 1899 he was made an Honorary Doctor of Letters of Oxford University, and St. Andrews University also similarly honored him. Finally, in 1905, King Edward VII himself named Meredith to receive the coveted Order of Merit, and with this, Meredith's aristocratic qualities were finally recognized by a formal designation. He died on the 18th of May, 1909, recognized by England in that year as one of her premier writers of the century.

What Meredith offers to us today is complex. We may have reservations about his possible deliberate concealment of his origins, depending on his motivation; a writer like Orwell would simply have said that Meredith had become a toady of the English aristocracy. But this is far from the truth. His life and work were consistent and if he did make a great error in his first marriage, it was an error of youthful exuberance, not of calculation. His strongest and most enduring works, in addition to the best of his poetry, would seem to be *The Ordeal of Richard Feverel*, *Evan Harrington*, *The Egoist*, and *Diana of the Crossways*, but perhaps there are as many as four other novels on nearly this same high level. *The Ordeal of Richard Feverel* is not only the logical novel with which to begin the study of Meredith, it is also perhaps his very strongest, in its unrevised and most spontaneous form - and in the following essays and commentary the present study will show how this great novel fits into the total pattern of Meredith's work.

THE ORDEAL OF RICHARD FEVEREL

INTRODUCTION TO GEORGE MEREDITH: THE RELATION OF MEREDITH'S FICTION TO HIS IDEAS

THE NOVEL OF PHILOSOPHICAL SATIRE

The object of this sketch is to treat a central group of six novels - a group which is representative of the larger body of Meredith's work. These are, in the order of their publication, *The Ordeal of Richard Feverel* (1859); *The Egoist* (1879); *The Tragic Comedians* (1880); *Evan Harrington* (1881); *Diana of the Crossways* (1885) and, finally, *The Amazing Marriage* (1895). It will be noted that these novels (if one omits the fantastic allegory, *The Shaving of Shagpat* [1855], from consideration as a novel) cover a chronological span from Meredith's earliest published novel to the last one published during his lifetime. In general, with the possible exception of *The Tragic Comedians* and *The Amazing Marriage*, they are the works of Meredith which have been most widely read and have received the most comment from the critics - not that, on an absolute scale, Meredith has ever been widely read.

These six major works will be considered in terms of their intellectual content and their artistic technique, and of the interaction between these two broad aspects of Meredith's fiction. Two critical documents which bear on both aspects-first, Meredith's lecture entitled *On the Idea of Comedy* and the *Uses of the Comic Spirit* (originally delivered in 1877, and hereafter referred to as the *Essay on the Comic Spirit*), and second, the "Preface" to *The Egoist* - are highly relevant to the works of fiction under discussion. Since Meredith is a novelist of ideas, passing in this respect beyond any of his contemporaries, except perhaps George Eliot, no treatment of his fiction can avoid discussing the nature and consistency of the ideas. For a concentrated statement of his chief ideas, one must turn briefly to representative poems of Meredith, as well as to the *Essay on the Comic Spirit*, and to his poetry in general (see essay below).

PREVIOUS CRITICISM

A few secondary sources have proved of some help in this study. Most conspicuous among these is Joseph Warren Beach's early book entitled *The Comic Spirit in George Meredith* (1911). Another helpful source is Chapter V of J. B. Priestley's *George Meredith* (1926); a chapter entitled "His attitude: The Comic Spirit." But secondary sources, usually, are not very helpful in the analysis of Meredith's art. The latest book-length biographical and critical study, *George Meredith: His Life and Work*, by Jack Lindsay (1956), is not really useful; it is choked with Marxist jargon, as witness the following:

> **Thus, he [Meredith] continued to admire Carlyle for his power to break through the thick falsities of their [i.e., the capitalists] world with a sharp phrase, a momentary depth of reactionary rage, his inability to relate his deep insights to the forward-movement of society through democratic struggle.**

One easily gathers that Mr. Lindsay forgets all about the objective Meredith for long stretches of his unintentionally amusing book, as he tries to make out a case for a Meredith who hated capitalism with a passion and hoped to bring in a society of "the workers" as a result of "the mass-movement of struggle." Interpretations of this sort evidence a complete inability to understand what Meredith was about. Meredith was a social critic, yes, but he believed that social regeneration and social progress lie within each individual; that a society is the sum of the men and women comprising it, which is a view hardly in keeping with orthodox Marxism. The word "egoism," which is often used by Meredith, is interpreted by Mr. Lindsay roughly as "capitalism." This book, although the latest, is one of the worst things which has been done on Meredith; yet the other criticism which is available is not really much more useful. Lionel Stevenson's book, *The Ordeal of George Meredith* (1953), is not well-documented and may be described as "superficial," but there is nothing better available in the way of a biographical and critical study, unless it is J. B. Priestley's book. Such a writer as Mr. Lindsay has been able to get away with advancing the silly theory that Meredith is a Marxist-oriented novelist simply because not much sound interpretation of Meredith has been done, recently or at any time in the past, and because Meredith is, on an absolute scale of judgment, a fairly "obscure" writer.

THE BIOGRAPHICAL PARADOX

Nor is the picture any more encouraging when we turned from the extant Meredith criticism to the biography. For, George Meredith, born an outsider to the upper social classes of Victorian England, endeavored, among other things, to mirror in his writing the manners of English ladies and gentlemen of his age. And he succeeded greatly because of the fact that as an outsider he could perceive distinctions and subtle gradations and behavior patterns which the possessors of land and wealth and titles and the "gift of a nine-hundred-year-old-name" simply took for granted. The body of his work bristles with titles: Lady Dunstane, General Ople, the Earl of Fleetwood, Lord Mountfalcon, Sir Willoughby Patterne, Colonel de Craye. The **themes** of his novels, as witness the autobiographical *Evan Harrington* or *The Tragic Comedians*, often involve the aspiration of a character to ascent in the social scale to the rank of the "Gentleman." It must be more than a coincidence that the situation of social aspiration in the novels is paralleled by the events of Meredith's own life history, the cardinal fact of which is that he was a driven man - driven to escape the stigma of the Portsmouth tailoring establishment from which the Meredith line sprang.

Meredith's life and work, then, is one great paradox, which has not even begun to be resolved by scholarship and criticism. A charge which may be leveled at Meredith is that he was nothing more than a social climber who ruthlessly clove his way to eminence by the only means then open to him - literature - the means by which another great commoner of "unfortunate" social origin, Benjamin Disraeli, made his way in the world. Stated in its strongest terms, the charge against Meredith might read: "Granted that Meredith is a difficult writer who had a lot to say about the England of his day and, by projection, about the world that was coming into being, he is not a trustworthy writer because he was basically insincere." A man who would speak of false snobbery and "Mammon-quakings dire as Earth's" in satiric terms; who would pillory the social pretensions and concealment of family background of such a figure as the Countess de Saldar (a thinly-disguised figure of one of his aunts) in *Evan Harrington*, while at the same time refusing to have anything to do with his father and lying about his birthplace and the source of his income on a trivial census form - how could such a man be sincere? Meredith, who could treat his wayward wife with a cold vindictiveness and make the ungentlemanly remark that there was a strain of madness in her family, while writing later with perception and sensitivity of the difficulties facing women in Victorian society, as represented by Diana Warwick and Carinthia Jane, is a bit too "paradoxical" for some readers to take. The point is that there exists an unresolved biographical problem here, which is most serious because quite a bit of Meredith's work, both in poetry and in fiction, has an autobiographical reference, and sometimes the screen which separates fiction from autobiography is of the thinnest gauge, as in *Evan Harrington*. There has been no definitive biography of Meredith, and consequently the assembly of the facts of his life must be done using the doubtful and imperfect method of consulting the books available, many of them bad or prejudiced, or both, along with reference to the Meredith letters and to accounts of Meredith's contemporaries.

Meredith, in terms of the content of both his poetry and his fiction, was a teacher as well as an entertainer. But he avoided even a hint of didacticism. As he wrote in *The Ordeal of Richard Feverel*:

The born preacher we feel instinctively to be our foe. He may do some good to the wretches that have been struck down, and lie gasping on the battle-field: he rouses deadly antagonism in the strong. Richard's nature, left to itself, wanted little more than an indication of the proper track, and when he said, "Tell me what I can do, Austin?" he had fought the best half of the battle.

SOCIAL NORMS AND THE COMIC MODE

Put another way, Meredith avoided "preaching" in his work through the use of a set of techniques which are comprehended by the name of the "Comic Mode." But he had a basically serious purpose: a coherent ideal, which he wished to promulgate, and a set of deviations from his ideal, which he attacked.

When one writes of Meredith's use of the Comic Mode, it is necessary to refer to "norms" or ideals toward which the use of comedy was pointed. Meredith was concerned with pointing out a way of life in which the individual could both realize his or her potentialities to the fullest and work for social progress at the same time. The intellectual basis of the Meredithian philosophy is to be found in the *Positivism of Auguste Comte*, the teachings of the earlier scientific evolutionists, and in other intellectual currents of the nineteenth century.

Meredith, in his fiction, mocked various departures from his "norm" of conduct: departures which may be assigned the names sensualism, asceticism, egoism, and sentimentalism. All through the novels we find these four vices pilloried. Their opposite seems to be a life lived in conformity with Nature; and for Meredith the concept of Nature had a special meaning, which we shall examine in a moment. Meredith used the rhetoric of the Comic Mode to attack the four vices or shortcomings listed, while removing the taint of conscious preaching or overt didacticism from his work. And how his techniques of fiction operate to define an ideal by indirection, while not seeming to be **didactic**, is the real subject of this sketch.

Meredith is not an easy author to read. His poetry is often marked by an extreme compression; his fiction often seems to drag horribly. The portrayal of actions is not his primary intention; rather, he analyzes the motives for action and the far-reaching results of action. *In The Tragic Comedians*, for example, a "history" based on the relationship of Ferdinand Lassalle and Helene von Donniges and the untimely and apparently pointless death of the former, Meredith tries to present an accurate, fictionalized account of the few crucial events in the lives of the "tragic comedians" that led to the death of Dr. Alvan, alias Ferdinand Lassalle. The significant actions in Meredith's novels are few, but one may find operating in them the concept of "the infinite moment" - the supreme moment" of choice in an individual's life - which is found not only in Meredith but also among his contemporaries, most notably, in the work of Browning and George Eliot.

Sentimentalism, egoism, asceticism, and sensualism: taken together, these four traits or behavior-patterns, represent the negative aspect of Meredithian moral dualism and imply the existence of a social and an individual ideal which was a very real thing for Meredith. It is useful to trace the pattern of these four negative traits as they operate in the six Meredith novels under discussion, in an effort to pin down the highly specific meanings Meredith had for these words, and to show the consistency of their use from one novel to another.

Meredith's attitude toward asceticism should be considered first, not because this was as all-inclusive or as damning a trait as egoism or sentimentalism for Meredith, but because in discussing asceticism and its opposite, sensualism, we will be able to move quickly into a systematic statement of the Meredithian evolutionary philosophy. Sensualism and asceticism are lesser defects, comprehended by the greater defects of egoism and sentimentalism in Meredith's ethical system; the two latter are so dangerous that they can destroy the individual and his society if not checked by the Meredithian corrective, *the Comic*

Spirit. When we have considered these four cardinal vices, we shall have developed the Meredithian ideal, defined in terms of its opposite.

MEREDITH'S RELIGIOUS OUTLOOK

Asceticism is, for Meredith, a worse crime against Nature than sensualism - in this view he runs counter to the official proclaimed morality of Victorian England. Moreover, Meredith early abandoned not only the supernatural elements in Christianity, after a brief flirtation while at the Moravian school at Neuwied; he also dismissed the basis of Christian ethics. For Meredith, the body was not something to be denied or to be disciplined; rather, it was to be harnessed in the service of the race. Meredith's ethics are more classical than Christian. One of the most contemptuous of all nineteenth-century literary references to Christianity occurs in the key Meredithian poem, *The Thrush in February*, a poem which compresses more of Meredith's essential thought into its lines than does any other work of his, whether poetry or fiction, as has been stated in the separate essay on Meredith's poetry:

> **I hear, I would the City heard.**
>
> **The City of the smoky fray;**
> **A prodded ox, it drags and moans:**
> **Its Morrow no man's child; its Day**
> **A vulture's morsel beaked to bones.**
>
> **It strives without a mark for strife;**
> **It feasts beside a famished host;**
> **The loose restraint of wanton life,**
> **That threatened penance in the ghost!**

The "famished host" is, in Meredith's view, the moribund Christian Church which had lost vitality and was in his time only going through the empty forms of religion. The "loose restraint of wanton life" - the denial of the body and the fear of hell - was really an outmoded and unnatural thing for Meredith, and he dismissed it. Yet he was the opposite of negativistic in this ethical theory. Like Shelley and Browning and George Eliot, Meredith had his own set of ethical standards, which, he believed, were more in keeping with natural law than was the "fading star" of Christianity.

FLEETWOOD

An example of the evil effects of asceticism is Lord Fleetwood, the "richest peer in England" and husband of Carinthia Jane, in *The Amazing Marriage*, who ended his days in sackcloth and ashes as the monk Brother Russett, who "perished of his own austerities." Lord Fleetwood is the character who most fully illustrates the destructive effects of asceticism, when compared with all the characters of the six novels under discussion. Fleetwood, it will be remembered, proposed marriage to Carinthia while dancing with her, and though he was not really serious about making her his wife, went through with the ceremony because, in conformity with the code of honor of the English Gentleman, he was always true to his word. But Fleetwood feared and despised what he considered the animal nature of women, as we see in this colloquy between the peer and the homespun philosopher and Meredithian "mouthpiece" Gower Woodseer:

> "Such animals these woman are! Good Lord," Fleetwood ejaculated. "I marry one, and I'm to take to reading medical books!" he yawned.

> "You speak that of women and pretend to love Nature," said Gower. "You hate Nature unless you have it served on a dish by your own cook. That's the way to the madhouse or the monastery. There we expiate the sin of sins. A man finds the woman of all women fitted to stick him in the soil, and trim and point him to grow, and she's an animal for her pains! The secret of your malady is, you've not yet, though you're on a healthy leap for the practices of Nature, hopped to the primary conception of what Nature means. Women are in and of Nature."

Notice the collocation of the words "madhouse" and "monastery." For Meredith, each was just about as bad as the other; the monastery symbolized that denial of the body, which Meredith found in Christianity and which, in his view, could only end in disaster both for the individual and for society.

SPECIAL ATTITUDES

In sharp contrast with Fleetwood's attitude toward woman is the relationship between Thomas Redworth and Diana Warwick, in the earlier novel, *Diana of the Crossways*. Redworth and Diana, after an inauspicious start, had both brought their lives into conformity with Nature. The doctrine of the moment of choice, or the "infinite moment," applies here. Diana made a mistake, which was understandable enough in view of the legal and social position of women in Victorian England, when she married Mr. Warwick. She made another mistake, nearly a disastrous one, when she was going to elope with Percy Dacier. Redworth made a mistake by not speaking out earlier for Diana. But neither of these characters was guilty of the Meredithian cardinal vices, and so had a chance at success in life. Redworth's relationship to Diana is described in Chapter XXXVII of *Diana of the Crossways* in these terms:

> She gave him comprehension of the meaning of love: a word in many mouths, not often explained. With her, wound in his idea of her, he perceived it to signify a new start in our existence, a finer shoot of the tree stoutly planted in good gross earth; the senses running their live sap, and the minds companioned, and the spirits made one by the whole - natured conjunction. In sooth, a happy prospect for the sons and daughters of Earth, divinely indicating more than happiness: the speeding of us, compact of what we are, between the ascetic rocks and the sensual whirlpools, to the creation of certain nobler races, now very dimly imagined.

The outcome of this book may sound like facile optimism: one places his or her life in conformity with something which Meredith called "Nature," and thereby attains success in life. But Meredith was anything but the "restless fool" of Matthew Arnold's poem in his view of Nature:

> "In harmony with Nature?" Restless fool,
> Who with such heat dost preach what were to thee,
> When true, the last impossibility -
> To be like Nature strong, like Nature cool!

For Meredith recognized the cruel aspects of Nature; the ending of *The Ordeal of Richard Feverel*, with the death of Lucy, should prove that. And Meredith recognized that Nature does not always offer a second chance to those who violate her laws. The "moment of choice" or the "infinite moment," once past, there is no possibility of recall, and sometimes entirely innocent people, such as Lucy, will suffer as the result of the rash choice of an egoist or an ascetic, such as Sir Austin Feverel.

Fleetwood freely chose to spurn his Carinthia, only to regret and repent after seeing proofs of her character. But it was too late for the proud peer, who died a monk. Fleetwood embodies the Meredithian vice of egoism as well as asceticism, as does Sir Willoughby Patterne, of *The Egoist*. Sir Austin Feverel has some elements of asceticism in his nature, in that his System is directed toward the repression of love, "the Apple-disease," with lamentable results, but in the group of novels here discussed, Meredith's best, the Earl of Fleetwood is the most conspicuous example of the Ascetic.

SENSUALISM

The opposite vice, sensualism, is possibly not quite as serious for Meredith as asceticism, for sensualism is a vice springing from the natural desires of the animal man: what Meredith called "blood" in his trinity of blood, brain, and spirit. The sensual appetites must be guided and harnessed by the higher powers of the body, but at least they are "natural," while conscious repression of the body and fear of the animal nature of man is a positive perversion in the view of Meredith. One of Meredith's key poems, in terms of its expression of his philosophy, was *The Woods of Westermain*, in which the following lines appear:

> **Blood and brain and spirit, three**
> **(Say the deepest gnomes of Earth),**
> **Join for true felicity.**
> **Are they parted, then expect**
> **Some one sailing will be wrecked:**
> **Separate hunting are they sped,**

> Scan the morsel coveted.
> Earth that Triad is: she hides
> Joy from him who that divides....

A frank sensualist is not nearly so dangerous a character for Meredith as a self-deceived sensualist, who, while believing himself to be "pure," in Victorian parlance, is actually a thinly-disguised brute. Possibly the closest thing to an open sensualist we have in the six novels is Adrian Harley, the "wise youth" of *The Ordeal of Richard Feverel*. Observe the operation of the word "discreetness" in this conversation between Sir Austin Feverel and Adrian over Sir Austin's program to ban Love at Raynham:

> "It only shows," said he [Sir Austin] how impossible it is to legislate where there are women!"
>
> "I do not object,' he added, "I hope I am too just to object to the exercise of their natural inclinations. All ask from them is discreetness."
>
> "Ay," said Adrian, whose discreetness was a marvel.
>
> "No gadding about in couples," continued the Baronet, "no kissing in public. Such occurrences no boy should witness. Whenever people of both sexes are thrown together, they will be silly, and where they are high-fed, uneducated, and barely occupied, it must be looked for as a matter of course. Let it be known that I only require discreetness."
>
> Discreetness, therefore, was instructed to reign at the Abbey. Under Adrian's able tuition, the fairest of its domestics acquired that virtue.

Adrian might be said to be an egoist, but he is of a less dangerous order than Sir Willoughby Patterne. For the wise youth is at least not self-deceived about his sensualism. He is "discreet," but his hedonism and sensualism are frank things in his own mind. Sir Willoughby, while congratulating himself that he is not as other men because, though they may be beastly in their attitudes toward women, he is "pure" and expects his wife to be spotless - Sir Willoughby is completely self-deceived as to the nature of his relationship with women. The sensualist is dangerous and socially destructive, but at least, like Adrian, he can be identified without too much trouble. The egoist is one thing, while he believes himself to be another. Much of Meredith's comedy arises out of the perception of this discrepancy between what the egoist and the sensualist are - and what they think they are.

The sensualist and the ascetic are, in general, the two lesser sinners for Meredith. Neither of them will contribute to race progress, and neither can fully realize his individual potentialities, which may be quite outstanding in all respects except for this one vice. The Earl of Fleetwood had many good qualities: he kept his word, he was a natural leader of men, and possessed an abundance of physical courage. In fact, in all respects save one he was the ideal English Gentleman, which Meredith sometimes seemed to put at the very peak of the evolutionary ladder, as can be shown in connection with a discussion of the Meredithian ideal as illustrated in *Evan Harrington*. But Fleetwood's positive virtues did not save him from a useless end. To die in a monk's cell may have been laudable for a medieval saint, or even for the Tennysonian Sir Lancelot. But for Meredith it was despicable: a shrinking from the upward movement of the race through evolutionary struggle. Fleetwood's was a vain life and a vainer death.

TECHNIQUE

It will be remembered that one of Meredith's unique techniques was his use of a mythical book of maxims or sayings interpolated into his novels; sayings which explain the action and in a way modify it. The most famous of these is, of course, "The Pilgrim's Scrip," in *The Ordeal of Richard Feverel*. In *The Amazing Marriage*, Captain Kirby, the Old Buccaneer, writes his "Maxims for Men." And in *Diana of the Crossways* we find Diana's sayings inscribed in the "Leaves from the Diary of Henry Wilmers." One is never certain whether these sayings reflect the opinions of Meredith himself, but the following, a saying of Diana from the "Leaves from the Diary of Henry Wilmers," is a representative expression of the Meredithian equation of man's life with Nature and with natural process:

> "A brown cone drops from the fir-tree before my window, nibbled green from the squirrel. Service is our destiny in life or in death. Then let it be my choice living to serve the living, and be fretted uncomplainingly. If I can assure myself of doing service I have my home within."

Sentiments similar to these were graven on Meredith's tomb: a quotation from the novel *Vittoria*:

> Our life is but a little holding, lent To do a mighty labour: we are one With heaven and the stars when it is spent To serve God's aim: else die we with the sun.

This is anything but the expression of a gushing and vapid philosophy of "service," to which latter-day philosophies, denying that one individual can do anything for anybody, are contemptuous rejoinders. The Meredithian ideal, as stated in the *Essay on the Comic Spirit*, involves the promotion of the welfare of society; *the Comic Spirit* exists to correct the vices we have been discussing and which are anti-social. In fact, Meredith once described *the Comic Spirit* as a social "disinfectant."

EGOISM AND SENTIMENTALISM

One must now turn to a discussion of the "greater" Meredithian vices of egoism and sentimentalism. We will then have the Meredithian cardinal vices and the Meredithian ideal partially defined, and will have made a start on the analysis of Meredith's artistic ordering of his intellectual content.

In the language of the law, sensualism and asceticism are "lesser included offenses" in the Meredithian major vices of egoism and sentimentalism. That is, elements of the lesser vices are comprehended in the greater. The Earl of Fleetwood and Adrian Harley are the type of the Meredithian ascetic and sensualist, respectively, although both of them partake of qualities which are included in the greater faults of egoism and sentimentalism. Adrian, we are told by Meredith, "made no pretenses. He did not solicit the favorable judgment of the world." Meredith, who, in *The Ordeal of Richard Feverel*, characterized sentimentalists as they "who seek to enjoy reality without incurring the immense debtorship for a thing done," might have called Adrian a sentimentalist except for the fact that at least he was not self-deceived. Adrian is a frank sensualist, while, in Diana's words, "The sentimental people ... fiddle harmonics on the strings of sensualism." Adrian is for himself alone, a sensualist, but at least he does not believe that he is doing his victims good, as does Sir Austin. Adrian's ambition was "to please himself, as being the best judge and, the absolute gainer." Now Sir Austin had no such ostensible ambition. In his view, since he was the deserted husband of a woman whom "he had raised to be his equal," he would live only for his son, and scientifically educate him to avoid the pitfalls of love. Such is the essential difference between the sensualist, Adrian, and the egoist sentimentalist, Sir Austin Feverel: the first man is conscious of what he is doing; the second is self-deceived. And the second is dangerous. It is not Adrian who caused the **catastrophe** which resulted in the death of Lucy. But Sir Austin is not a good subject in whom to illustrate the workings of sentimentalism and egoism; there are more clear-cut cases in other Meredithian novels.

THE TRAGIC COMEDIANS

In The Tragic Comedians we find a clear-cut example of a self-deceived egoist and because Dr. Alvan has few of the intricacies of Sir Willoughby Patterne in his character, I shall consider him first. Dr. Alvan, a socialist and a Jew, was doubly repulsive to the parents of Clotilde, and, initially, to Clotilde herself. She gradually became attracted to Alvan because, prior to their meeting, many of her intellectual friends remarked on how similar her social and political and philosophical views were those of Alvan. Their meeting is the start of a passionate love-affair, for they seem to have an elective affinity for each other. Alvan's first words to her betray the mark of the great egoist, although it is only fair to say that Alvan has a lot more to be egoistic about than does Sir Willoughby Patterne. Alvan had heard many times prior to their meeting of the brilliant woman whose opinions and personality were so like his, and he says to Clotilde: "You are she! - so, then, is a contradiction of me to be the commencement?" Clotilde had just expressed disagreement about a theory of Alvan's when the latter first spoke to her.

Alvan is a much more real character than the Marquis de Sidonia, of Disraeli's Coningsby, that other lofty Jew of nineteenth-century British fiction. He is a natural leader, and so brave and skilled with weapons that his refusal to duel, on moral grounds, is not interpreted as cowardice. He is one of the most powerful men in Europe, and upon his life hinges the life and progress of the country. Yet all this is brought low in a duel. Alvan is killed by a chance bullet fired by the fool, Prince Marko, after contemptuously firing his own pistol into the air. And Clotilde survives, only to take the inexplicable step of marrying Marko, the killer of her lover Alvan.

Meredith wrote, in *Modern Love*, the following oft-quoted lines:

> **The wrong is mixed. In tragic life, God wot,**
> **No villain need be! Passions spin the plot;**
> **We are betrayed by what is false within.**

This quotation may be brought to bear on the central situations of much of Meredith's fiction, and especially does it apply to *The Tragic Comedians*. For it is something false within that betrayed Alvan, and that something was egoism. Marko Romaris is only the accidental instrument of his destruction. Alvan's egoism finally leads him to be untrue to himself. "Why will you not rise to my level and fear nothing?" Alvan asks Clotilde. But when she finally determines to break with her bigoted family and run away with her lover, it is Alvan himself who, by choosing to become "respectable," is the agent of his own destruction. Meredith's concluding comment is interesting:

> **He was neither fool nor madman, nor man to be adored: his last temptation caught him in the season before he had subdued his blood, and among the**

> multitudinously simple of this world, stamped him a tragic comedian: that is, a grand pretender, a self-deceiver, one of the lively ludicrous, whom we cannot laugh at, but must contemplate to distinguish where this character strikes the note of discord with life-for otherwise, in the reflection of their history, life will seem a thing demoniacally inclined by fits to antic and dive into gulfs. The character of the hosts of men are of the simple order of the comic; not many are of a stature and a complexity calling for the junction of the two Muses to name them.

Sigismund Alvan was culpable because he was tempted to make himself socially acceptable to Christian aristocrats of the stamp of Clotilde's parents; he was too blind to see (as Clotilde was not) that his refusal to take her, except as a Christian gentleman presumably would, "at chirche door" and with the blessing of her parents, meant nothing to the furiously bigoted General von Rudiger. Alvan's character is torn apart: "the two men composing it, the untamed and the candidate for citizenship, in mutual dissension pulled it down. He perished of his weakness, but it was a strong man who fell.... A stormy blood made wreck of a splendid intelligence." T. S. Eliot's lines from *Murder in the Cathedral*, apply here:

> The last temptation is the greatest treason:
> To do the right deed for the wrong reason.

By attempting to do "the right deed," Alvan violated his essential nature. With regard to his marriage with Clotilde, "he aimed at standing well with the world and being one with it honorably." But Alvan was by nature a rebel, fitted to smash existing social lies and contribute to the progress of his country. In the last analysis, it was egoism which led Alvan to wish to stand well with a stale social order (Mr. Lindsay would no doubt describe it as a "capitalist-reactionary" society), as represented by Clotilde's father and by Marko Romaris.

Two sides of Meredith's own character are reflected by that of Sigismund Ivan, which may be a reason for Meredith's interest in the historical events of Ferdinand Lassalle's life and death. Meredith saw social progress as coming through strife, but he always held "the rapture of the forward view." He believed in the certainty of evolution, but was never so rash as to attempt to predict the direction or goal of this evolutionary process. But he is far from the iron economic determinism of Marxism. In fact, he was an aristocrat by aspiration and achievement, if not by birth, although he was capable of writing such poems as Juggling Jerry and The Old Chartist, and of refusing an Order of Merit at the height of his success. The ideal "English Gentleman" represented a positive force for good in the world, and Meredith wished to be classed with him. Marx's views on the gentry and the aristocracy were hardly so complimentary.

THE EGOIST

One turns now to the complex figure of Sir Willoughby Patterne, egoist and sentimentalist, who, because of Meredith's exhaustive examination of his spiritual and intellectual self-deception, is probably the most representative Meredithian antihero. It is often said of *The Egoist* that it is a boring novel in which nothing ever happens, that the most "exciting" point in the action comes when Clara Middleton takes her "flight in wild weather" to the railway station, and after a spell of indecision, returns. What suspense! Will she or will she not take the train? It is apparent that action plays an even lesser part in the fabric of *The Egoist* than it does in most Meredithian novels, and, since the two-volume Memorial Edition of this novel runs to 626 pages, it is not surprising that *The Egoist* should appear to drag.

Joseph Warren Beach analyzed the character of Sir Willoughby Patterne in these terms:

> **Sir Willoughby made dishonest use of the natural passion of love to cover another order of passions. He is the most broadly typical of Meredith's figures, and illustrates the essential divorce from nature of the civilized egoist. The thorough egoist is incapable of the passion of love in its full sense. For the grand passion requires a forgetfulness of self, a surrender of the limited interests of the individual to the larger purposes of nature. The grand passion does not select its object with deliberate calculation of the worldly advantage involved.... Sir Willoughby wished a wife who would be worthy of the station she must assume as his lady. In choosing Clara Middleton he could see the telescopes of all gentlemen turned enviously upon his moon. This is not the way of the grand passion.**

Sir Willoughby is both an egoist and a sentimentalist, which is probably why Professor Beach characterized him as "the most broadly typical of Meredith's figures." Yet, his activities do not appear to lead to any catastrophic result; this is in contrast to Sir Austin Feveral, Lord Fleetwood, and Dr. Alvan. Nevertheless, Sir Willoughby encompasses the characteristic of the latter Meredithian "tragic comedians." Sir Willoughby is a most dangerous man because he is self-deceived. As Regan said of her father, Lear, "he hath ever but slenderly known himself." This line, a key to much of Shakespearean tragedy, may be brought to bear on the self-deceived comic heroes of Meredith's novels, and the outcome of their lives may be potentially as tragic as the lives of Lear or Macbeth or Othello. Sir Willoughby believes that he is full of regard for the welfare of his intended bride; he congratulates himself that in this respect, as in everything, he is "not a other men are."

THE OBJECTIVES

In Meredith's "Prelude" to *The Egoist*, the objectives of this novel are outlined, even though the author entitles this section, "A Chapter of Which the Last Page Only is of Any Importance," after the fashion of Fielding, who in Tom Jones used to treat his critical prefaces in a politely deprecatory manner. "Comedy," Meredith wrote, "is a game played to throw reflections upon social life, and it deals with human nature in the drawing-room of civilized men and women, where we have no dust of the struggling outer world, no mire, no violent crashes, to make the correctness of the representation convincing."

So much for the lack of action in the Meredithian novel. As a matter of fact, this preliminary chapter of *The Egoist* is almost as important as the *Essay on the Comic Spirit* for an understanding of Meredith's purpose and technique. "The spirit born of our united social intelligence...is the Comic Spirit." Now, Willoughby is at odds with "our united social intelligence" from the first, as were Adrian Harley and Sir Austin Feverel and indeed every one of the Meredithian anti-heroes, in one way or another. Meredith continues in his "Preface":

Now the world is possessed of a certain big book, the biggest book on earth; that might indeed be called the Book of Earth; whose title is the Book of Egoism, and it is a book full of the world's wisdom.... Art is

the specific. We have little to learn of apes, and they may be left. The chief consideration for us is, what particular practice of Art in letters is the best for the perusal of the Book of our common wisdom; so that with clearer minds and livelier manners we may escape, as it were, into daylight and song from a land of fog-horns.

Sir Willoughby's doings are inscribed in this *Book of Egoism*, but he is the last person in the world to realize this. Both Adrian's calculating hedonism and Sir Willoughby's egoism are unnatural, in terms of the Meredithian philosophy of nature. But Sir Willoughby is much the more dangerous person. Let us look at just one scene from the first part of *The Egoist* to illustrate Sir Willoughby's self-deception, and the pillorying of it by the Comic Spirit.

The vital scene takes place in Chapter VI, entitled "His Courtship." The dialogue is between Clara Middleton and Sir Willoughby. "He was indefatigable in his lectures on the aesthetics of love," Meredith tells us. This is the mark of the sentimentalist, "who would enjoy reality without incurring the immense debtorship for the thing done." Constant talk about a love which is sentimental and anti-social in nature smacks of the egoist who would disregard the social implications, the social utility, of his behavior.

Sir Willoughby congratulates himself that he is a prince among men as he discourses of love to Clara. He finds a delicious pain-pleasure as he contemplates the fact that in every married couple, one person will die before the other. He imagines what the fate of Clara would be were he to die suddenly:

"Is it any wonder that I have my feeling for the world? This hand! - the thought is horrible. You would be surrounded; men are brutes; the scent of unfaithfulness excites them, overjoys them. And I helpless! I see a ring of monkeys grinning. There is your beauty, and man's delight in desecrating. You would be worried night and day to quit my name to... I feel the blow now. You would have no rest for them, nothing to cling to without your oath."

"An oath!" said Miss Middleton.

And the oath which Sir Willoughby wishes his betrothed to swear is no less than this:

"An oath?" she said, and moved her lips to recall what she might have said and forgotten. "To what? what oath?"

"That you will be true to me dead as well as living! Whisper it."

"Willoughby, I shall be true to my vows at the altar."

"To me! me!"

"It will be to you."

"To my soul. No heaven can be for me - I see none, only torture, unless I have your word, Clara. I trust it. I will trust it implicitly. My confidence in you is absolute."

Here Sir Willoughby shows himself to be at once an egoist and a sentimentalist. He is an egoist because he has no real regard for Clara Middleton as a person; he wishes complete and absolute possession. In the phrase used by John Stuart Mill in his essay *On the Subjection of Women*, it is not sufficient for the Victorian husband to have his wife a slave; she must be "a willing slave." Sir Willoughby demands that his wife surrender to him to such an extent that she will swear fidelity even after death. The truth is that Sir Willoughby regards his wife as a form of property, and he is tormented by the thought that other men encroach upon his property. One is reminded of Diana's saying: "Men may have rounded Seraglio Point: they have not yet doubled Cape Turk." While congratulating himself on his consideration and respect for Clara's wishes, Willoughby actually shows himself to have the attitude which a Turk or an Indian chief ostensibly has toward his woman. What is this but the mark of the supreme self-deceived egoist?

Further, Sir Willoughby is a sentimentalist by virtue of the fact that he luxuriates in the pleasing melancholy of the feelings occasioned by the possibility of his early demise. The reaction of Clara Middleton to this stuff is the reaction of any healthy-minded individual to an abnormal delight in melancholy. What Sir Willoughby wants is such absolute possession that his wife will no longer have an individuality of her own; thus, under all the professions of ideal purity peeps the unregenerate man. Sir Willoughby truly "fiddles harmonics on the strings of sensualism."

UNIQUENESS

Meredith's selection of the sentimentalist and the egoist, especially the sentimentalist, for the target of comic artistic treatment is unique in the history of the English novel. The remarkable thing about Meredith's writing is that it seldom or never angers us by didacticism, by attempting to push his ideas down our throats. Yet the fiction is loaded with ideas. Essentially, Meredith is successful in the avoidance of overt didacticism because he cleverly, by the use of his art, sets up a situation in which the characters who represent Meredithian cardinal vices convict themselves out of their own mouths.

Put another way, Meredith avoided "preaching" in his work through the use of a set of techniques that are comprehended by the name of the Comic Mode. When direct preaching seems to take place, it is soon found to be "loaded" in such a way that it rebounds on the preacher himself. For example, many of the sententiae of "The Pilgrim's Scrip" actually become ironic comments that convict Sir Austin Feverel right out of his own mouth. "Life is a tedious process of learning we are Fools.... When we know ourselves Fools, we are already something better." This is the dangerous sort of verbal wisdom which can lead its possessor to say, with the Pharisee in the Eighteenth Chapter of the Gospel According to St. Luke: "God, I thank thee, that I am not as other men are, extortioners, unjust, adulterers, or even as this publican." We know from reading *The Ordeal of Richard Feverel* what this "wisdom" results in. Sir Austin Feverel is a more dangerous man than Adrian Harley primarily because he is self-deceived, like the Pharisee. His System would go against the laws of Nature, and being imposed on a boy of Richard's natural spirit, leads to destruction for a perfectly innocent person. And still Sir Austin does not realize his own guilt - far from the conventional villain of fiction who repents at the end.

MEREDITH'S ETHICS AND PHILOSOPHY

Of Meredith's preoccupation with sentimentalism: his classing it with egoism as among the cardinal sins can only be explained in terms of his philosophical principles. If one does not understand these, it is difficult to see why Meredith went to such elaborate lengths to forge his techniques of the Comic Spirit in order to attack these social evils. Meredith would attack the sentimentalist and the egoist because, turning inward instead of outward, they make no contribution to society or to the progress of the race. The Meredithian ideal of Service is well expressed by the conclusion of *The Amazing Marriage*, the late novel which focused many of Meredith's ideals.

Carinthia Jane, becoming a nurse, went off to Spain and "nursed Carlists and Legitimists alike" in the wars. Here we find a combination of the aristocratic ethic of noblesse oblige and the duty of service imposed by the law of nature. One should turn once again to *The Thrush in February*, where Meredith, in referring to Nature, wrote:

> **She judged of shrinking nerves, appears**
> **A Mother whom no cry can melt;**
> **But read her past desires and fears,**
> **The letters on her breast are spelt.**
>
> **A slayer, yes, as when she pressed**
> **Her savage to the slaughter-heaps,**
> **To sacrifice she prompts her best:**
> **She reaps them as the sower reaps.**
>
> **But read her thought to speed the race,**
> **And stars rush forth of blackest night:**
> **You chill not at a cold embrace**
> **To come, nor dread a dubious might.**
>
> **Her double visage, double voice,**
> **In oneness rise to quench the doubt.**
> **This breath, her gift, has only choice**
> **Of service, breathe we in or out.**

> Since Pain and Pleasure on each hand
> Led our wild steps from slimy rock
> To yonder sweeps of gardenland,
> We breathe but to be sword or block.

These five **stanzas** should go far to refute the charge against Meredith that he was arbitrary and even cruel as he worked out the resolution of such a novel as *The Ordeal of Richard Feverel* or perhaps *The Amazing Marriage*. Sentimentalism would say that Lucy is the last person who "should," in terms of her moral deserts, suffer because of the perversity of Sir Austin Feverel. Sentimentalism would seek "another chance" for Lord Fleetwood. But Meredith, under the impact of the idea of competitive evolution as well as guided by common sense, realized that Nature is cruel and unforgiving if we misread her; that one mistake can result in a grand **catastrophe** as in a Shakespearean tragedy, or in the death of Lucy Feveral or Sigismund Alvan. "Service is our destiny in life or in death," said Diana. We are here to develop ourselves and to speed the progress of the race, and what happens to us in the process is of no account. The two concluding **stanzas** of *The Thrush in February* are as strong an expression of this idea as may be found anywhere in Meredith's writings:

> For love we Earth, then serve we all;
> Her mystic secret then is ours:
> We fall, or view our treasures fall,
> Unclouded, as beholds her flowers.
>
> Earth, from a night of frosty wreck,
> Enrobed in morning's mounted fire,
> When lowly, with a broken neck,
> The crocus lays her cheek to mire.

For Meredith, the central question which the orthodox Christian asks is: "What shall I do to be saved?", with the emphasis on the "I." This would seem another form of egoism to Meredith; his views regarding the necessity of self-forgetfulness and of service thus account for the quality of religious sanctions in his work.

COMEDY

It is in *An Essay on Comedy* and the *Uses of the Comic Spirit* that Meredith pointed out both the techniques and the purposes of his art. "Purposes" by design, for Meredith, while shunning overt didacticism, was far removed from the critical school of Pater and "Art for Art's sake." A criticism of Meredith's Essay is furnished by Professor Beach, who writes:

> **In his famous Essay Meredith was not so much reviewing the practice of the comic art as attempting to shadow forth the method in which he was at work himself. His effort to illustrate his meaning was somewhat pitiful.... He would have been more intelligible had he drawn his illustrations from his own novels. He must have been sore tempted to do so. One might suppose that the "Egoist," which appeared two years after the lecture was delivered, was offered to show what he had in mind.**

Doubtless Meredith would have done better to have explained what he was doing by using illustrations from his own novels, rather than by referring to Congreve or Cervantes. But Meredith was trying, among other things, to prove the universality of the Comic Spirit and the social need of it, and in this cause he drew examples from world literature. He may have felt that people would have thought him presumptuous had he analyzed his own works in the Essay.

Meredith's essay has as its full title: "On the Idea of Comedy and of the Uses of the Comic Spirit." The small word that is too often overlooked here is uses. The **theme** of the work seems to be that the Comic Spirit serves a social purpose, and that few works of real comedy as a social corrective have been written. The intellectual content, or "philosophy" of Meredith's novels, is best approached through the poetry. And the form which these novels took, the method of artistic ordering, is best approached through this Essay.

Meredith believed that comedy was impossible of attainment in a society which assigned an inferior or servile place to women. He sets up a hierarchy of races and nations in terms of their relative sinfulness in this respect, saying of the Eastern lands:

> **Eastward you have total silence of comedy among a people intensely susceptible to laughter, as the Arabian Nights will testify. Where the veil is over women's faces, you cannot have society, without which the senses are barbarous and the Comic Spirit is driven to the gutters of grossness to slake its thirst. Arabs in this respect are worse than Italians - much worse than Germans - just in the degree that their system of treating women is worse.**

VIEW OF SOCIETY

Now Meredith was not writing this to bring about a reformation of society in the Arab countries. What he is really driving at is a reconsideration of the function of the Comic Spirit at home.

He says himself: "I am not quoting the Arab to exhort and disturb the somnolent East; rather for cultivated women to recognize that the comic Muse is one of their best friends. They are blind to their interests in swelling the ranks of the sentimentalists."

Meredith attacked the Germans for lacking the Comic Spirit. He admired many characteristics of this nation, and we must not overlook the fact that he spent two impressionable years in Germany in his youth. But his final judgment was that "the poor voice allowed to women in German domestic life will account for the absence of comic dialogues reflecting upon life in that land." For a commentary which will go far to explain what Meredith was talking about in his criticism of various national groups in terms of their lack of comic perception, one might look at the collection of short stories and sketches entitled *In a German Pension*, by Katherine Mansfield. These stories were written during the period 1909–1911, and were based on experiences which Katherine Mansfield underwent some thirty-three years after Meredith delivered the lecture on the Comic Spirit in 1877. Taken as a group, these stories present a picture of a land where women are little better than domestic animals, and where men, in consequence of their dictatorial powers, "wax out of proportion, overblown, affected, pretentious, bombastical, hypocritical, pedantic, fantastically delicate... self-deceived... drifting into vanities, congregating in absurdities..." Or so these qualities were described in the Meredithian language of the *Essay on the Comic Spirit*. Of the Germans Meredith said: "The discipline of the Comic Spirit is needful to their growth." Even here, Meredith is not so much censuring a given nation as he is pointing out a universal ideal.

We must discuss *Evan Harrington*, finally; a work which has been deferred until now because in it the comments about the Meredith biography will fall into a pattern and help to explain the characteristic problems raised in Meredith's art. *Evan Harrington* is the most autobiographical of Meredith's novels.

In the person of the Countess de Saldar, alias Lou Harrington, the tailor's daughter, we have the best example in Meredith's work of a snob. Now snobbery is a form of self-deception akin to sentimentalism, in that it takes outward shows for inner realities. The comic element consists in the constant danger which the snob or the pretender to social position finds himself in: the danger of exposure. As soon as a man or woman begins to congratulate himself on his superiority to the common herd, we have snobbery. Sentimentalists are snobs in spiritual things. Sir Willoughby was this kind of snob, as well as being the common or garden variety (as in his treatment of the poor naval officer who is the father of Crossjay Patterne). The spiritual snob, or sentimentalist, is always congratulating himself on the fact that his perceptions and feelings are finer than those of ordinary men. Sir Willoughby's insistence on his fine feelings to Clara is snobbish.

George Meredith himself was both a snob and a sentimentalist, elements in his character which led J. B. Priestley to characterize him, in the conclusion of his biography, as "A genuine poet and philosopher, on the heroic plan, who can dwindle at times into a mere fop; a rich genius in whom there is some curious streak of the shoddy adventurer; a man of Shakespearean mold crossed with a strain of a Beau Brummell." In a sense, like the saloon-keeper who drank himself into bankruptcy, Meredith was his own best customer. He wrote the story of his early life, idealized to be sure, in *Evan Harrington*. All the members of his immediate family appear in the novel, and the shadow of his grandfather, Melchisedek Meredith, constantly reminds us of the origins of the Meredith house. But none of this was known until after Meredith's death, so cleverly did he conceal his social origins.

THE ENGLISH GENTLEMAN AND COURTESY LITERATURE

Part of Meredith's prolixity in books such as *Evan Harrington* and *The Egoist* can be explained only in terms of his personal preoccupation with the doctrine of the English Gentleman. English courtesy-literature has its immediate origins in the Italian Renaissance, and the best known English documents in this form are probably Sir Thomas Elyot's *Book of the Governor* and, in the eighteenth century, the Earl of Chesterfield's *Letters to his Son*. Courtesy-literature in general took up such topics as these:

1. What is a Gentleman?
2. The Theory of the Favored Class
3. Occupations for the Gentleman
4. The Moral Code of the Gentleman
5. The Education of the Gentleman
6. Which studies are of the most Worth?
7. Exercise and Recreation

A question of primary importance in courtesy-literature was whether or not a Gentleman must be of gentle birth. Another question involved the social utility of the Gentleman. It is obvious that no society will continue to support a class which contributes nothing to that society. Meredith's near-contemporary, Carlyle, recognized this and, in Past and Present most notably, tried to recall England's hereditary aristocracy to a sense of its social duty, which was anything but the right to "go gracefully idle in Mayfair." Newman (in *The Idea of a University*, Discourse VIII), Arnold, Disraeli, and other Victorian writers, whether poets, novelists, or essayists, concerned themselves with the British aristocracy and its changing obligations in society.

Ruth Kelso, the writer of the best scholarly work on the English tradition of the Gentleman, says this of the social utility of that class:

> **The justification and therefore the existence of any privileged class rests ultimately upon its serviceableness to the community. When the core is gone, though the shell may for long exist intact, the whole body is doomed sooner or later to decay. The core of European nobility as a class - that is, as a group possessing from generation to generation certain definite privileges - went with the passing of the feudal system and the development of strong, central authorities, and national as distinguished from baronial warfare.**

Meredith's aristocratic ethic stressed the ideal of service. This view of the function of the English Gentleman was based on analogy with the physical universe: "the army of unalterable law," to take a line from one of Meredith's better-known sonnets. Diana's statement: "Service is our destiny in death or in life" is, it might be said, the application of the physical laws of the conservation of matter and the conservation of energy to the sphere of social relations and of ethics.

Meredith set up a philosophical ideal in his poetry and in the *Essay on the Comic Spirit*. The ideal operates, in its various aspects, in Meredith's fiction. Those who do not conform to the teachings of natural law - Sir Austin, Dr. Alvan, Lord Fleetwood, and above all, Sir Willoughby Patterne - become comic characters in their self-deception. But what happens to them - or worse, what happens to other innocent people as a result of their egoism or sentimentalism - is far from comic.

Meredith's ideal was empirically-based, rather than based on the reading of books. As he would have said: "I read the Book of Nature," leaving his audience to violate the laws of Nature at their peril. It must be remembered that the courtesy-book tradition itself sprang from observation of social manners, even as did Meredith's novels and his philosophical view of Comedy. It was descriptive rather than prescriptive writing, and it tried to point out an idea based on the best practice, the best conduct, the best English Gentleman.

EVAN HARRINGTON

Let us look at the action of *Evan Harrington* to see how this works in practice. Melchisedek Meredith, though a tailor, had some most untailorly traits. He was buried, one remembers, in the uniform of a lieutenant of militia dragoons. Military service as an officer has always been one mark of the English Gentleman. Melchisedek was a tailor, and was never known to have sent a bill. Liberality in money matters is a second important trait of the English Gentleman. Now Melchisedek's daughters had, by marriage, all risen in the social scale. But in their hidden pasts the shadow of the shears - a trade peculiarly despised in Victorian England - was something to be concealed. The efforts of the brilliant Countess de Saldar to disguise her social origin becomes a study in high comedy. Meredith constantly plays with the idea that it is conduct and manner, rather than birth or superficial appearance, which certifies to the true English Gentleman. All through the novel, Evan, the tailor's son, is contrasted favorably with Lord Laxley, his competitor for the hand of Rose Jocelyn. Toward the beginning of the novel, Evan quarrels with the snobbish and empty-headed Lord Laxley at an inn, and there is almost a duel. But Evan does not try to conceal the fact that his father was a tailor, and Lord Laxley contemptuously refuses to duel with him. Part of the code of the Gentleman specified that duels could take place only between social equals; a Gentleman would demand himself by dueling with a tradesman. Ideally, this meant that a Gentleman had to stand ready to account for his words to his social equals, but a member of the "lower classes" was exempt from such a duty. The point is that Evan conducted himself so well that the company believed that he was in fact a Gentleman:

> **Sit down, and don't dare to spoil the fun any more. You a tailor! Who'll believe it? You're a nobleman in disguise.**

At the end of the novel Rose Jocelyn, who has been engaged finally to marry Lord Laxley, wishes to be released in order to marry Evan. The ramifications which led to the admission on the part of Rose's aristocratic family that Evan might be a fit mate for Rose, after all, are not particularly important here. But the final judgment on Lord Laxley, the born aristocrat, is significant:

> **The behavior of Lord Laxley in refusing to surrender a young lady who declared that her heart was with another exceeds all I could have supposed. One of the noble peers among his ancestors must have been a pig!**

In the last analysis it is Evan who proves by his conduct that he is the better Gentleman. Meredith examined the concept of gentility from every conceivable angle, and the conclusion that he undoubtedly wished to arrive at, that it is possible for one who has not been born an English Gentleman to become one, and conversely, that it is possible for one who has been born a Duke to behave in a swinish manner - this conclusion shines through all the pages of *Evan Harrington*. It is what Meredith, who strove all his life to be considered a Gentleman, wished to believe, and it colored every page of his fiction.

MEREDITH'S IDEALS

There is, then, in Meredith's writing, and certainly in the group of six novels which have briefly been considered here, a tension that has hardly been pointed out as yet: a tension between the use of high comedy to point out the ways in which the race might grow spiritually, and the conscious avoidance of didacticism on Meredith's part. His ideals are all defined by indirection, but they are certainly present, for if anyone in Victorian England wrote the novel of ideas it was Meredith.

In order to have comedy one must first have an ideal: a point of reference which operates to make departures from it capable of comic treatment. Meredith had such a point of reference and it was made up of a philosophical view of Nature rising by degrees to Spirit, along with a definite social ideal: an aristocratic ethic of social service which was colored through by the doctrine of the English Gentleman. Meredith's point of reference, of course, partakes of what Meredith himself was, his social origins and aspirations.

Finally, Meredithian Comedy has a use, which is to give man greater self-knowledge. All the Meredithian cardinal vices - asceticism, sensualism, egoism, and sentimentalism - stem from inadequate self-knowledge, which is clearly demonstrated by the characters who embody these vices and convict themselves out of their own mouths. Comedy ideally will bring about a society of men who have attained self-knowledge, and it will be impossible for them to be guilty of the negative and anti-social traits which the Meredithian comic corrective attacked:

> They, hearing History speak, of what men were,
> And have become, are wise. The gain is great
> In vision and solidity; it lives.

Such is Meredith's social ideal, and such is the method by which he sought its actualization.

INTRODUCTION TO THE ORDEAL OF RICHARD FEVEREL

A PRELIMINARY NOTE

The novel is divided into forty-nine Chapters, and the most logical way for our Detailed Commentary and Summary to proceed is by the order of these Chapters. The Ordeal has a dramatic structure and could well be reduced to dramatic form and acted as a tragedy or tragicomedy, but most likely as the former, because of the darkly tragic outcome of the Richard-Lucy relationship. It is modeled, probably by clear design on the part of Meredith, on the romantic tragedy of Shakespeare, *Romeo and Juliet*. Readers have sometimes felt that the book has a curiously unsatisfactory ending. After all, the novel, like Samuel Butler's *The Way of All Flesh*, Goethe's *The Sorrows of Young Werther*, Hardy's *Jude the Obscure* (see Bright Notes Study Guide, by the present author), Joyce's *Portrait of the Artist as a Young Man*, is in the tradition of the "Novel of Development," or Bildungsroman, which - invariably centers around the efforts of a young man to "find himself" and to understand, if not himself, then at least the world in which he finds himself. A characteristic of such a novel is a period of "storm and stress," which sometimes culminates happily, as in the case of Ernest Pontifex as he wins through to a state of relative maturity and competence, in Butler's novel.

But *The Ordeal of Richard Feverel* falls somewhat outside the Bildungsroman tradition, unless one can overcome, or at least neglect, the very harsh and stark ending, in which the innocent die. What will Richard's future be? Can one imagine any future for him, young as he is, as a product of his father's "system" of education? One must devote time to a careful reading of *The Ordeal* to clarify such a question, and then, the answer may still be unsatisfactory.

RECEPTION

The Ordeal of Richard Feverel, all things considered, is a great novel, and remains so under the possible erosion of the reputation of the Victorian novel under the pressure of time and of changing social patterns. It was not well received upon original publication, but then, for precisely that reason - its starkness and **"realism"** of outlook on the relationship between the sexes - it has been better thought of in our own century. Meredith put more of himself into this novel than into any of the others, or indeed even into his poetry, with the exception of *Modern Love*. This work, a marital tragedy, is a fine quasi-sonnet-sequence which chronicled, as also in part did *The Ordeal*, the disaster of Meredith's own first marriage, with all the consequences which this unhappy relationship entailed for Meredith.

Furthermore, Meredith put more of his philosophy into this book than into any of his other novels. He did embody many of his ideas in *The Egoist*, *Diana of the Crossways*, and *Evan Harrington*, but none of these works really seem to have proceeded from as deep an emotional and unconscious level as did *The Ordeal*. For this was not only Richard Feverel's Ordeal, it was also that of Meredith himself.

The writing is characterized by a combination of intellectualism, **satire**, and sheer poetry. Of nineteenth-century English novelists, Meredith is undoubtedly the outstanding practitioner of the poetic novel, for he was basically, as the essay on Meredith's poetry included in this study has tried to show, a poet: a poet of ideas, and a poet of Love. His poetic vision leads, sometimes, to difficulties in communication with the reader of his fiction. He adopts the method of poetry: compression and symbolic statement, rich **imagery** beyond what fiction can ordinarily sustain; subtlety of shading in tone. In the fantastic seduction scene in Chapter XLII, "An Enchantress," the relationship between Richard and Mrs. Bella Mount is treated imagistically in terms of the infernal regions. Richard, as a result, not of the fall from grace which he undergoes, but from his lack of ability to handle this sophisticated and worldly situation, ultimately comes to grief - and it is a scene that is in a sense as much a poetically treated "Descent into the Underworld" as is Meredith's great poetic forebear's scene: the Cave of Mammon, in Book II of Edmund Spenser's *The Faerie Queene*.

PLOT AND ACTION

A brief discussion of the plot and action of *The Ordeal of Richard Feverel* is in order at this point. Most commentators on the novel have perceived that the plot is rather closely related to that of Shakespeare's first major tragedy, *Romeo and Juliet*; in fact, plot and characterization are almost parallel in Shakespeare's play and in Meredith's novel. There is abundant evidence that Meredith is literally steeped in Shakespeare; in *The Ordeal*, for example, one of the crucial scenes has the title, "Ferdinand and Miranda," and of course this refers to the young lovers in Shakespeare's magic play, *The Tempest*. But the darkening tendency of the plot of Meredith's novel, culminating in a **catastrophe** which does have tragic force, is that of Shakespearean tragedy rather than that of Shakespearean philosophical romance, into which latter tradition *The Tempest* falls. The only ray of hope in the ending of *The Ordeal* lies in Meredith's doctrine of philosophical vitalism; his belief that Life itself is or can be heroic, and that the life of any particular individual is of importance only in terms of the larger picture of the life and progress of humanity itself. But as we contemplate the tragic ending of *The Ordeal*, with its death of the innocent, we may have a difficult time accepting Meredith's hard doctrine, as he himself anticipated.

The scene in *The Ordeal*, "Ferdinand and Miranda" (Chapter XVIII, in which Richard falls in love with Lucy at first sight, may impress the reader as not typical of the reserve and repression thought to be present in English Victorian society. But, actually, such an event is quite within the Victorian belief in the power and, indeed, the supreme worth of Love, with the partners in such a great romantic drama being able to discern each other instantly - the doctrine of "elective affinities," as Browning illustrated it in his poems such as *The Last Ride Together*, *Count Gismond*, and in his masterpiece, *The Ring and the Book*. And this is associated with a companion Browning doctrine: the doctrine of the Infinite Moment, whereby through a soul's free choice, the future state of that soul as well as, it might be, his or her state in this life, is irrevocably determined. Such a choice is made by Giuseppi Capponsacchi, Browning's hero, in *The Ring and the Book*, as he confronts for the first time the heroine, the girl Pompilia.

MEREDITH'S NATURALISM

Meredith holds a number of the same views as his great poetic contemporary, Browning, but the two part company on the point of Christian orthodoxy, for Meredith's orientation is naturalistic rather than what might be called supernaturalistic. This is one of the reasons for the powerful and moving nature of the tragedy of Richard Feverel: there is no comforting notion of an Afterlife, as there is in Browning's poetry, in which all will be well. Meredith's anti-sentimentalism, vitalism (the doctrine that the processes of life are not explicable by the laws of physics and chemistry alone, and that life is in some part self-determining, opposed to mechanism) and philosophical naturalism - terms which we shall explain in a Meredithian context presently - are a bit removed from the main temper of the Victorian age; but they give Meredith, at his best - and *The Ordeal of Richard Feverel* is his best - a tragic force and a compelling power which appeals to the sense of reality of our own century to a greater extent, it may be, than can be the case of such great Victorian writers of fiction, more popular in their own age, as Dickens and Thackeray. But let us turn to the plot of Meredith's great novel to see what manner of tragedy it is.

Richard Feverel is the only son and heir of an English baronet (in England a baronet is one who is just below the grade of the peerage; it is a degree of honor just below a baron, and above a knight. While a baronet is a commoner, not a nobleman, he is entitled to have "Sir" prefixed to his name, but he does not have the hereditary right to sit in the House of Lords, nor is he addressed as "Lord") who lives on an estate in one of the western counties of England. Richard's father, Sir Austin Feverel, has decided to bring up his son according to a System of education he has developed himself; a System which has a rather strange ethical and moral orientation, leaving little room for passions and emotions and regarding Woman as a snare and a danger for man. This apparently ascetic discipline, which Meredith refers to throughout the novel as "the System," is the result of Sir Austin's own very unhappy marriage to a lady, Richard's mother, who had run off with his best friend, Denzil Somers, who seems to have been a failed artist and a treacherous as well as a weak friend and guest. Not perceiving that part of the fault for this debacle lay with Sir Austin himself, the baronet had blamed it all on the nature of Woman, and had tried to remove his son from this baleful influence.

This portion of *The Ordeal* is cut from autobiography; Meredith's own marriage, as we have seen from his biography, having turned out in this manner, had wounded his pride very deeply so that it took him a long time to recover, if indeed he ever did. His first wife, Mary Ellen, had left him in 1858, leaving him with a five-year-old son. *The Ordeal of Richard Feverel*, the writing of which began rather soon after the flight of Meredith's wife, appeared in October, 1859, that Annus Mirabilis, or "wonderful year" of English literature and letters of the nineteenth century, which also saw the publication of one of the volumes of Ruskin's *Modern Painters*, John Stuart Mill's most famous essay, *On Liberty*, part of Tennyson's *Idylls of the King*, Thackeray's *The Virginians*, Dickens' *A Tale of Two Cities*, part of Carlyle's *Frederick The Great*, which embodied additional evidence for Carlyle's view of the place of the Hero in history, and finally, perhaps the most important book of the century published in England by an Englishman, Charles Darwin's *The Origin of Species*.

While Darwin's great scientific work appeared in November, a month after *The Ordeal of Richard Feverel*, the idea of evolution through Natural Selection had been in the air for perhaps two-thirds of a century previously. Darwin's was the most noteworthy and most definitive statement of this key idea. Meredith had absorbed such ideas, and by the time he came to write *The Ordeal*, he was fully cognizant of the latest theories of Natural Selection, although it cannot be said that Darwin's book "influenced" him directly, in view of the dating of the two works.

THE SYSTEM

The **catastrophe** of *The Ordeal of Richard Feverel*, then, would seem to proceed in great part from the kind of "unnatural" education which the System provided Richard - the System leading to thwarting of sound natural impulse, and in turn ultimately to the defeat of the progress of the race. Meredith seemed to regard mankind, the human race, as evolving and dynamic, with man in the position of making free moral choices which could help or hinder this process.

Now, Sir Austin Feverel's System was a hindrance, stemming from deficiencies in Sir Austin's personality and makeup which he in turn unconsciously attempted to inflict on his son. The tragedy of the book - the unbearable final section of it - consists in the suffering of the perfectly innocent. But all great Western tragedy, whether Greek or Elizabethan or the more doubtful tragedy of later eras, portrays the suffering of the innocent as well as the guilty. Nietzsche described tragedy as "the re-affirmation of the will to live in the face of death," and while *The Ordeal of Richard Feverel* ends tragically, yet, in Meredith's view, there is at least a re-affirmation of the will of the race (we are more cautious, with good reason, about the exaltation even of the concept of race than was a nineteenth-century writer such as Meredith) the will of the race to endure and to transcend itself. The ultimate meaning of much of the outwardly simple, Romeo-and-Juliet story of *The Ordeal of Richard Feverel* lies in Meredith's philosophical poetry, which is the subject of a separate essay in this Guide, and it may be observed that

The Ordeal is being read in the light of the ideas of Meredithian poetry, though it is a self-subsistent work of fiction.

The intent of the System, then, is to bring up Richard in a discipline which will insure that he cannot be harmed by Woman. Ultimately, the psychological roots of the System would seem to lie in Sir Austin's own inadequacies; by bringing up his son according to such a System, he will prove in some way that he, Sir Austin, was right and his wife was wrong in the relationship which had led Sir Austin to disaster. Thus, he is not training his son as a unique and sovereign personality, but rather as an object for experiment. From this primal offense, the tragic action will proceed.

Lest one think that the idea of such a System of education and training is far-fetched, he has only to look at the lives of a number of illustrious figures in nineteenth-century England. John Stuart Mill, as he tells us in his famous Autobiography, was given such an education, according to a system, by his father, the brilliant philosopher and public official; it was an education which began him on Latin, Greek, Logic, Mathematics, and other abstruse and difficult subjects at a very early age - but which neglected the emotions completely. As a result, Mill had a serious breakdown around his twenty-first birthday and was for a time on the verge of suicide; he rescued himself, typically, by putting himself through a course of reading the Romantic poets, especially Wordsworth. But he himself regarded the System as something from which he barely escaped with his life. So it will be with Richard Feverel.

Many of Sir Austin Feverel's philosophical aphorisms, descriptive of the System and of his views on Woman and related subjects, are contained in a book of sayings which he had published anonymously under the title of *The Pilgrim's*

Scrip. These aphorisms are quite important, not only showing Sir Austin's views, but also in indicating the distance between appearance and reality in his own case. For Sir Austin is a dangerously self-deceived man. Meredith often uses such a book of maxims - a book within a book - as a literary device for authorial commentary without direct moralizing.

Sir Austin has a widowed sister, Mrs. Doria Forey, who serves both as a participator in the action and a kind of chorus. And there is, in his household, also Adrian Harley, called frequently "the wise youth"; he is an Epicurean quasi-philosopher who loves pleasure. He had graduated from a University with the idea of becoming a clergyman, but instead had become a protégé of his uncle, Sir Austin, and served him as a general handyman in the intellectual and social spheres. It is Adrian's job to attend to the education of Richard, although he has serious doubts about the System, believing it to be against human nature.

This ménage lives at Raynham Abbey (called an Abbey, incidentally, not because there is a religious foundation of monks living there - except perhaps in Meredith's satirical view of Sir Austin's ascetic System - but rather because there once had been such an establishment there, probably dissolved in the sixteenth century, during which time King Henry VIII and several of his successors deeded over land, belonging originally to Church foundations, to a new class of landholding aristocracy.) There is, in the establishment, also Benson, the butler, nicknamed "Heavy" Benson, who has some of the hatred of women of Sir Austin. Also, there is Ripton Thompson, the son of an old family friend and family attorney of the Feverels, who has been imported because Sir Austin feels that Richard needs such companionship. Richard's cousin, Clare Doria Forey, has been destined by her mother to marry Richard, but instead, Clare will be unwillingly married to a man twice her age and will die very young. She, too, is in a sense a victim of a System, treated not as a sovereign person but as an object by which personal advantage may be obtained by her mother. Clare is the counterpart to Richard, and her ending, while from an artistic point of view rather contrived, is analogous to what happens in Richard's case.

In the chapter entitled "Ferdinand and Miranda" (Chapter XVIII), Richard meets for the first time the simple and breathlessly beautiful country girl, Lucy Desborough, falls instantly in love with her, presently elopes, and marries her secretly and without the consent of Sir Austin. An effort of the family is made for purely selfish reasons, disguised by religious and social prejudices (Lucy is of a Catholic family, and her people are farmers, not aristocracy). Clare's mother also attempts to prevent this marriage because she wants Richard for Clare. From this point, the golden and most poetic glow of this spring romance deepens and darkens, as does the love affair in Romeo and Juliet, "too sudden...too like the lightning."

The book darkens into the winter of a bitter tragedy of young love and young idealism, uncontaminated by worldly knowledge, but unable to defend itself because of the pernicious effects of Sir Austin's System on Richard. The net result of the interference of the family is to separate Richard and Lucy - Richard having an increasing sense of guilt over his behavior toward his wife. Richard is seduced by an experienced and designing young woman, Mrs. Mount, the "Enchantress" of Chapter XLII. This leads Richard to feel even more unworthy. Meanwhile, the attempted seduction of Lucy by a dissolute English peer, Lord Mountfalcon, with the assistance of his pandering parasite, the Honorable Peter Brayder, is not successful. Lucy would never hear of it, especially as she is by then expecting Richard's child.

Richard and Lucy's son is born, and then Richard finds out, just as he is being reconciled to his father and his wife, of the nobleman's attempted seduction of Lucy. He, of course, hot-bloodedly challenges Mountfalcon to a duel; this takes place and Richard is wounded, although not dangerously. He is on the way to recovery when his wife and father finally arrive to be with him, but Lucy's health cannot stand any more of the great strain which has callously been imposed on it from all sides, including most conspicuously Sir Austin's System. Lucy becomes very ill from "cerebral fever," and just as Richard is at the point of recovery from his wounds, she lapses into a final coma and delirium and dies. And this final scene, with the tragic death of the young mother who leaves Richard with their son, but desolate, is almost unbearably poignant, for Meredith understates what could else become as sentimental as a scene in one of Dickens' less distinguished novels. Meredith writes a young man's tragedy here, but a tragedy which ascends to almost archetypal significance; it is the story pertaining to the greatest possible troubles of the life of a young man, not of a mature one. And the tragedy, paradoxically, comes about directly by Richard's innocence and naivety, and indirectly by Sir Austin's unconsciously vicious System, which has not quipped Richard to deal with the problems which all men must face. It is as though the children of light, which Richard and Lucy are, as are Ferdinand and Miranda, do not understand the pseudo-wisdom of the children of the world, such as the Wise Youth, Adrian, and must pay the price for this laudable but fatal lack of understanding, whether they are guilty or, like Lucy, completely innocent. For the world extracts a heavy price in these matters, sometimes amounting to the very lives of those who by any standard or test deserve better. One questions whether, at the ambiguous ending of *The Ordeal*, Richard, even with the resilience of the young, will ever be able to recover; artistically, Meredith leaves this up in the air, for reasons which can be perceived as we turn to our detailed consideration of the novel.

THE ORDEAL OF RICHARD FEVEREL

TEXTUAL ANALYSIS

CHAPTERS 1-10

CHAPTER I: THE PILGRIM'S SCRIP

The Pilgrim's Scrip is an anonymously-published book containing a number of wise, even brilliant-sounding aphorisms and maxims, lacking charity, according to some readers of the book, and mostly on the subject of Woman. Rather typical of these sayings are, "I am happy when I know my neighbor's vice," and "Life is a tedious process of learning we are Fools." These two, the very first in the volume, have great relevance to the case of Sir Austin Feverel, father of the hero of the novel, Richard, for they ironically describe Sir Austin. And there is a third: "I expect that Woman will be the last thing civilized by Man."

There is no signature; instead the sign, or coat-of-arms, of a Griffin between Two Wheatsheaves appears on the volume. By investigation on the part of some of the readers of the book, mostly female, it is discovered that the arms of a Griffin between Two Wheatsheaves is the family crest of Sir Austin Absworthy

Bearne Feverel, Baronet of Raynham Abbey, in "a certain Western County folding Thames." This information had actually been discovered by investigation at the College of Heralds, where a record of all coats of arms is maintained. (A Griffin is a mythological monster, half-lion and half-eagle.) After his identity is established, Sir Austin receives visitors at Raynham Abbey, mostly women coming to attempt to persuade him that his indictment of Woman's nature is wrong.

The author of *The Pilgrim's Scrip* observes to his nephew and confidant, the "wise youth," Adrian Harley, that "it is odd that, when we whip her, Madam should love us the more." Adrian calls *The Pilgrim's Scrip* "The Great Shaddock Dogma," which is a rather sophisticated reference to the Fall of Man in the Garden of Eden, as recounted in Genesis. We learn, subsequently, that even while Sir Austin is being paid attention by a number of ladies who have come to Raynham to attempt to get him to change his mind about their sex, a System of education for his only son and heir, Richard, is being developed. The essence of Sir Austin's System is that he would teach his son to live "scientifically," for if enough men could do this, a new Golden Age would result in which the human race would be free of the ills, evils, and diseases which mortality involves. Sir Austin had studied human nature with a scientific eye, knowing what a "science" it is to live. He proposes to institute his Golden Age by hedging his son from the corruptions of Life, and at the same time promoting his health; he would develop innocent of the evils represented by the symbolic eating of the Apple from the Tree of Knowledge in the Garden of Eden. This is the germ of the tragedy that is to eventuate as a result of Richard's education according to the System; it is established as early as the first part of the first chapter of the novel. In Meredith's view, Sir Austin is attempting to do what simply cannot be done, to change human nature suddenly by a doctrinaire effort. He is looking at mankind "scientifically," and emphasizing "brain," the rational faculty, over the other two faculties which Meredith sees in Man's makeup; what he calls "blood," or the animal nature, and "spirit," or what he calls or would consider the faculty that makes Man in truth what he should be, but only if spirit is conjoined to blood and brain:

> **Blood and Brain and Spirit**
> **These Three**
> **(Say the deepest gnomes of Earth)**
> **Join for true felicity....**

So Meredith wrote, in his philosophical poem, *The Woods of Westermain*.

In the first chapter, then, is the perceptible beginning of that which has been foreshadowed at the moment when Sir Austin decides to preserve his son from the "Apple-Disease," another reference to the Original Sin, as visited by womankind on Man in the Garden of Eden when he eats of the apple, the forbidden fruit.

Comment: A rather profound commentary on the first chapter of the *The Ordeal of Richard Feverel* is contained in one of the very finest poems, "XXX," of *Modern Love*, discussed in the essay on Meredith's poetry elsewhere in the present Guide, and printed following the long poem, *The Thrush in February*. In line 15 of "XXX" of *Modern Love*, Meredith refers to "the scientific animals." But while the word "scientific" has a plus-value for our own era, Meredith's use of it is not without some ambiguity of meaning. It is not a word of unqualified praise in the case of Sir Austin, for he looks at human nature to learn the science of living, but not its art.

Sir Austin ruins not so much his own life, for that is already embittered, but that of his son, with his "scientific" theories of which the System is the bitter fruit. Indirectly, in Chapter I, but certainly with subtlety, the character of Austin Feverel is developed, and we learn what can be expected of him. Second, the chapter established rather quickly and with reasonable economy, considering Meredith's elliptical and poetic way of telling or implying a story, the genesis of Richard's Ordeal. His Ordeal is not Woman, but rather his father's System of education. We already see that Richard is being made into an object rather than a subject, a being whose existence and whose education according to a rigid System is intended to prove something and to justify Sir Austin to himself. The story really has begun in medias res, thus partaking of the nature of drama, which always must begin in this manner; we do not yet know why Sir Austin wishes to educate Richard according to a System, or why he professes to despise women. But the answers to these questions about Sir Austin are revealed in the second chapter.

CHAPTER II: A GLIMPSE BEHIND THE MASK

The genealogy of the Feverels - the name had originally been spelled Fiervarelle, in the Norman French manner - is humorously treated in this chapter, but under the humor we can see the wound which had been dealt Sir Austin and which is responsible for his wish to impose his System on Richard. The Welsh tend, in English literature, to be treated somewhat humorously; although Meredith himself was of Welsh origin, he continued this tradition. They were thought to be great storytellers and great exaggerators, and one remembers Shakespeare's flamboyant Welsh characters, such as Captain Fluellen and Owen Glendower, in the *Henry IV* and *Henry V* plays.

A good part of the material in this chapter, besides the genealogy, is political and historical, and requires for its full understanding some knowledge of English history; it is not, however, absolutely essential to the narrative. But with a family such as the Feverels, their descent and social setting do help to show what they are. Sir Austin had been in Parliament, on the Tory side, as his landowning interests would by and large have dictated in the nineteenth century, and had been well thought of by his constituents in his County, where he is one of the principal men; the County, incidentally, is probably identifiable as Somersetshire. Suddenly, something had happened to Sir Austin; he had given up his place in political life and become practically a hermit. He had decided that the Feverels were somehow doomed by heredity to undergo "ordeals."

Sir Austin's story was actually one of the oldest in the world: "He had a wife, and he had a friend. His marriage was for love; his wife was a beauty; his friend was a poet." The friend was named Denzil Somers, with whom Austin had become acquainted at College; he was indeed nominally an artist and a poet, who had published his early poems under the pseudonym of Diaper Sandoe (it not being quite respectable, perhaps, to publish them under his own name). Somers had been Sir Austin's perpetual house guest and companion at Raynham because he was not well-off financially. Put bluntly, Somers was a sponger, in more ways than one; he had been extravagant and spent such money as he had inherited.

Lady Feverel was "of no particular family," says Meredith; she was the daughter of a naval officer who had educated her while he was retired at half-pay. This seems a very snobbish attitude, but we shall see why Meredith was rather venomous in his description of both Somers and the lady. After five years of marriage, and twelve years of friendship with Somers, Sir Austin, whom we may infer by this would - have been a man of perhaps thirty-three to thirty-five, imperious and used to having his own way, was left with neither wife nor friend, but only his infant son, Richard. For Somers and Lady Feverel had simply run away together one day. While Sir Austin could bring himself to forgive his friend, whom he regarded as weak in the extreme, he could not forgive his wife, whom he had, as he saw the case, "raised to be his equal," and she had betrayed him.

Comment: Sir Austin belonged to the landholding aristocracy of nineteenth-century England, and thus was in an exceptionally favored position. Under the English law of primogeniture (inheritance of the eldest, or first-born) the oldest son of a family would inherit not only a title, if any, but also all of the property and the estate. Sir Austin was thus wealthy and socially respected and seemed to have been of an outgoing nature until the tremendous blow to his pride occasioned by the departure of his wife with the despised poet-artist.

The truth is that this account of the wife's conduct is something in which Meredith was emotionally involved, for Meredith's first wife had, as we have seen from his biography, done exactly this sort of thing, and there is much more to the case than meets the eye. There is an implication that the cold superiority and pride of Sir Austin had driven his wife to do this thing. Reading the character of Sir Austin in this manner, it is possible to find a hidden

element of satirical autobiography in this novel which adds an additional dimension to its meaning. Sir Austin took the kind of cold revenge on his wife which Meredith had taken on his own estranged, runaway wife Mary Ellen, although at the time when *The Ordeal* was written, Meredith did not know what tragedy would subsequently strike his wife, abandoned by her lover.

Sir Austin had become stern, cold, and reserved, and as a sign of his inner turmoil, had started walking in his sleep and was greatly troubled. He dismissed a servant girl who had seen him doing this, but to the world he appeared distant and self-possessed, bearing his "troubles" well. But the psychological picture of him presented by Meredith is that of a deeply disturbed man who had never before suffered such a reverse.

"In youth I looked out from under a hail of blows," wrote Meredith of himself later, when he was a successful and famous writer. But *The Ordeal* had been written in the heat of the moment of his betrayal by his wife; and, indeed, was his reaction to that event; this is one of the aspects of this novel which accounts for Meredith's great achievement in it, because it was written from his own deeply felt experience.

Few authors begin their literary careers by writing a great masterpiece, to which their future works are by and large anti-climactic. But this seems to have been Meredith's case, and one explanation of the situation may well be that Meredith was more personally involved here than in his other fictions, except for

Evan Harrington, which is less romantic and more satirical. But we shall consider this point further.

CHAPTER III: MRS. MALEDICTION

Meredith may have seemed wordy, but it is true that by the end of the second chapter of *The Ordeal of Richard Feverel*, he has very skillfully sketched out the characters of the Feverel family, and established the motivation for what will be the tragic action of the book.

In Chapter III, the scene is laid in the Hall of the Feverels at Raynham Abbey, when the family gets together to celebrate Richard's birthday. The boy's uncles, "Algernon, the guardsman, Cuthbert, the sailor, Vivian, the diplomatist and beau," make a point of coming because the Baronet, at once their elder brother and the head of the family, has among other things the control of the purse-strings; his younger brothers have gone into professions of suitable station and honorableness for gentlemen to pursue: Army, Navy, and the Diplomatic Service. Mr. Justice Harley, an in-law, and Colonel Wentworth, another in-law of the Feverel family, propose toasts to the young heir (again, the notion of the Gentleman's profession, the Law and the Army). But at this point, Richard is still young and is not yet being actively shaped by his father's System.

Soon thereafter, Richard has a strange dream in which a woman appears to him in his sleep and kisses him on his forehead, but does not speak. Sir Austin is alarmed. Perhaps it is a supernatural visitation - but really, he knows what it is: the return of Richard's estranged mother who had wished to see her son.

Richard is to be examined medically at his father's orders, to see if he is sound (really, if he is in condition to begin the training which the System demands). But here, at seven, he shows the first hint of self-will when he refuses to submit to the medical examination. His father, of course, prevails on him. Colonel Wentworth has perceived that the boy was indeed visited by a woman, but he does not tell Sir Austin that the woman was Richard's mother. Anyway, Sir Austin probably knows this subconsciously.

Comment: This chapter is relatively straightforward, except for the hint of supernatural visitation, which has a quite natural explanation. But the meaning of this chapter involves more than might appear on the surface, in terms of the psychology of Sir Austin. He has been as guilty as his wife in the proceeding which led to her running off with Somers. But he represses this guilt under a stern and cold pride, which is his ultimate offense.

Just as Henry James used the theme of vampirism - officious meddling in the affairs of others - as a primary motif in his works, so Meredith uses it in his histories of the soul. The Vampire, whether in Meredith or in James, feeds on his victims while maintaining the illusion that he is doing them good. So Sir Austin treats Richard, even to forcing him to submit to a medical examination, though he is healthy enough. Essentially, he is treating Richard as a thing, not a person; he has a vested property right in Richard - so he seems to feel - and thus he must see how his property is faring. Richard, after all, is the heir to the fortune and to Raynham. But he is also an independent and inviolable personality, and this Sir Austin does not sufficiently regard or respect.

CHAPTER IV: THE INMATES OF RAYNHAM ABBEY

Even the title should give a clue to the rather zany originals who inhabit the Abbey presided over by Sir Austin. Meredith presents them in the light of "humorous" characters (using the term "humor" in its sixteenth- and seventeenth-century meaning of a character who is motivated by some rather abnormal or grotesque trait, ultimately traceable to physiology). Mrs. Doria Forey is introduced here as one of the Feverel relatives who is to play a large part in Richard's life. She is one of the three sisters of Sir Austin, and had married a younger son of an aristocratic family who expected that he might inherit a fortune but died before this could take place, leaving his wife with one child, a daughter. Mrs. Forey, widowed and with no financial means, had contrived to get herself invited to Raynham by her brother, and there she stayed. She regarded his experiment with a System of education as nonsense, but had the circumspection to keep her opinions to herself at this point, for what she wanted was something that would make it possible to retain the good opinion of Sir Austin. Besides, she was solely dependent on her brother for support. She had determined that her daughter, Clare, was to marry Richard and become the heiress of Raynham, even though Clare and Richard were cousins.

Austin Wentworth also is a resident of Raynham; he is the son of Colonel Wentworth, an in-law of the family. He had committed the awful deed of "marrying his mother's housemaid," and therefore the young Austin Wentworth had become something of a family black sheep, though he is naturally of a noble, almost saintly, character in comparison with most of those at Raynham. Richard's father, who along with Mrs. Forey rather admires Austin Wentworth for his independence, still treats him rather severely, because after all he had betrayed the concept of family honor.

The "wise youth," Adrian Harley, has as his principle "to satisfy his appetites without rashly staking his character." Adrian wishes to enjoy himself without being committed to people; he is a pleasure-loving lone wolf, who does not make any pretenses as to what he is. He likes to eat, and, in general, enjoys all pleasures of a non-intellectual nature. Heavy Benson, the butler, is surly and misogynistic as the result, apparently, of an unhappy marriage.

Thus, each of the characters at Raynham, except Richard, has something the matter with his character or personality or physical constitution. Only Richard, the inheritor of "good blood" and uncorrupted by the kind of experiences which had befallen the others, seems healthy; in fact, he bubbles over with health, so that Sir Austin's friend, the doctor, is called in to prescribe for him. The doctor wisely suggests companionship of Richard's own age and, in accordance with this sound advice, Sir Austin selects Ripton Thompson, son of the family solicitor (actually a lawyer the solicitor would not be considered anywhere near the social rank of Sir Austin, as he deals primarily with routine matters of property administration). Ripton is invited to Raynham, on probation as it were, but fits in well and stays as Richard's companion.

Comment: The System begins to operate, for in this chapter Richard grows from his seventh to his fourteenth birthday. The doctor is consulted again, and this is really an ironic twist, for we can see from this chapter that all of the inhabitants of Raynham, save the child Richard alone, have been wounded. Only Richard is normal, and the System, with the best apparent motives, is very likely to end up by making Richard similar to all of the others in Raynham. This is clearly implied, even as early as the third and

fourth chapters of the work. At this point, the doctor and Sir Austin talk seriously about the possibility of Richard's marrying, and Sir Austin says that Richard will not marry until he is at least thirty. One can guess that Richard would, in Sir Austin's view, be better off not marrying at all, except that if there is no heir to Raynham, the fortune and the estate might pass into other hands than those of the direct line of the Feverels, and this would be unthinkable to Sir Austin. So Sir Austin plans that Richard will marry, but at a time suitable to the family, not to Richard. This is the first decision of the System. The doctor rather obliquely informs Sir Austin that the System will not work, because it is against nature, but Sir Austin chooses not to listen.

CHAPTER V: THE FOURTEENTH BIRTHDAY

On his fourteenth birthday, Fate has decided to try Richard and the System together at the impartial bar of Nature. Richard and Ripton decide to go hunting, even as the neighboring townspeople are coming to Raynham to help their patron celebrate the birthday of the heir to the manor. Richard calls his friend Ripton a fool, for no good reason, and they decide to fight, which they do in the wood, with Ripton having the worst of the battle. Afterward they make up, and Richard agrees to say that Ripton is not a fool.

After this exchange, they move onto the lands of the neighboring farmer Blaize, who is no friend of the Feverels, and Richard shoots at a pheasant. Now, in rural England even at this point in the nineteenth century, poaching is serious business, and farmer Blaize is within his rights when he orders the boys to give up the bird they had shot on his land. They refuse, or rather the high-spirited Richard refuses, and Blaize begins to horsewhip them until they give up the bird and leave his land in some haste. But Richard vows revenge. He thinks of various ways in which he can get the better of the farmer who had whipped him. There are implications in his reaction to this incident; he takes it too seriously, and Meredith implies that this is the fault of the System. After all, what Richard and Ripton had been doing while hunting uninvited on Blaize's land was a crime, a crime which earlier in English history could have entailed very severe punishment, even death.

> **Comment: This scene explains something which had happened earlier to Richard and which he had reacted to violently when he announced that he had been insulted. It is the work of the System, Meredith implies, that Richard's reaction to this ordinary reverse of life is quite disproportionate to the thing itself - but the artificial upbringing created by the System has led Richard to this reaction, which is to be the first such evidence of the System's failure. Richard is in the wrong, but he does not perceive this, and Ripton, as he will hereafter, is content to believe what Richard believes and to follow his lead.**

CHAPTER VI: THE MAGIAN CONFLICT

The title of this chapter takes its name from the conflict in Richard's mind between his desire for revenge and the partial perception that perhaps he was wrong in the incident of farmer Blaize. The Magus (wise man; sage) Zoroaster was the great religious teacher of the Persians and the founder of Zoroastrianism. Now, this religion is quite dualistic; its basic tenet is that in the created world there is a ceaseless conflict between Good, personified as the god Ormuzd, the principle of good, and Evil, personified as the god Ahriman. Unlike the theology of Christianity, where the issue between God and Satan is never really in doubt, at least in most Christian sectarian views - the theology of Zoroastrianism seems to imply that the issue has not been decided, whether by predestination or by chance or by positive actions.

What the conflict is in this chapter is between the forces of Ormuzd and Ahriman within the breast of Richard Feverel. Will he do good, or will he do evil by an attempt at revenge upon Farmer Blaize. This is an outwardly humorous situation, but with a core of serious meaning. The whipping of a boy of fourteen for poaching may seem well-deserved, but the point is not in the event itself. It is in Richard's reaction to that whipping. He does not accept it with good grace, as he should, because he is in the wrong. Put this way, the comment is naive, but still, Richard's reaction is disproportionate. As the chapter ends, Richard has bargained for a loaf of bread with a Tinker (a pot-mender, considered a low social type in the England of the period) and with his assistant, Speed-the-Plough, humorously named. The latter has said of "Varmer Blaize... I should like to stick a Lucifer in his rick soam dry windy night." This refers to the offense of rick-burning - to set on fire the farmer's hay-rick, or pile of hay, which might end up by burning him out. As the chapter ends, it seems that Richard has his idea for revenge. He will have a rick-burning somehow on Blaize's farm. Ahriman has won!

Comment: In Zoroastrianism, it was man's high duty to cooperate with the forces of Good in bringing the entire universe under the domain of Ormuzd, god of the Light. The dark powers constantly attempt to upset this balance, and to gain the upper hand.

There are two points which will be developed in this discussion of Meredith, but which should be noted here briefly: (1) Meredith's father-in-law, the humorous and satirical English novelist, Thomas Love Peacock, was very much interested in Zoroastrianism, for a friend of Peacock's, John Frank Newton, was what might be described as another interesting English grotesque, a practicing Zoroastrian. (2) Meredith used much Zoroastrian imagery in *The Ordeal of Richard Feverel*. Thus, it becomes a suggestive idea that what Meredith may have been writing about was an evenly-balanced warfare between Good and Evil in this novel, with the scales really balanced so that the latter, Ahriman - or call it simply the forces of disorder in the universe - will win, or have the distinct possibility of winning. And this is, in the highest sense, a subversive idea, subversive in terms of what the entire Western Judeo-Christian intellectual and ethical tradition stands for.

Even this early in the book, then, we may begin to realize that its ethical orientation is not in the main line of its century; it can really be described as unique.

CHAPTER VII: ARSON

After The Magian Conflict, it is but a logical step to the carrying out of Richard's plan for revenge. At the birthday party, the place of honor is vacant, and Sir Austin assumes that Richard has defied him. Many members of the family have ulterior motives in coming to see Richard on his birthday; they are interested in what Sir Austin can do for them, not in Richard. One cousin brings her daughter, the lady Juliana Jaye, a young girl, hoping to catch Richard's eye and lead to an arranged marriage. Richard will be a very good catch for any girl, because of his prospects and his inheritance. By ten o'clock, Richard still has not appeared.

Under the humorous or half-humorous view which Meredith seems to take of the battle for Richard and his inheritance, there is a serious purpose. Richard is once again being treated as an object, not as a personality, by his relatives. His father is already treating him so, because Richard's training by the System is supposed to prove the rightness of Sir Austin's cause. As to the fact of Arson in this scene, Adrian Harley, the wise youth, perceives that some mischief is afoot when he says to Richard: "I'm perfectly aware that Zoroaster is not dead. You have been listening to a common creed. Drink the Fire-worshippers, if you will."

There is a double meaning here, as in so many of the lines in *The Ordeal of Richard Feverel*. Adrian is alluding to the Magian, or Zoroastrian, conflict; a Zoroastrian sect were the Parsees, who were fire-worshippers. Richard is testing out this conflict, in his own person, between Ormuzd and Ahriman. Thus, by a process of imagistic circumlocution, Richard Feverel's revenge, or planned revenge, on Farmer Blaize, is described. While Adrian thinks of Sir Austin as "a monomaniac," he keeps his opinion to himself.

Sir Austin finds that Richard is absent from his bedroom, and overhears him talking to Ripton about a plot which seems to involve a Tom Bakewell. They are waiting for something. Presently in the distance, in the valley, there is a flame. To be blunt, Richard has paid Tom Bakewell a guinea (one shilling more than an English pound) to set Blaize's hay-ricks on fire. Clare also overhears them, and faints as they look gloatingly on the fire they have set at a distance with no risk to themselves - so both Clare and Sir Austen are in on the secret.

> **Comment: It is important that Sir Austin know this early the first result of his System. Richard has done what is essentially a cowardly act, and the System evidently has not worked. Why, then, does Sir Austin persist? We know even at this early stage that Sir Austin will persist in his folly until something much worse happens. Rick-burning, treated half-humorously here, as stated, is a very serious crime in rural England, and the only result of the System has been to lead Richard to do this thing without thought of the consequences and without the realization that he may be in the wrong.**

CHAPTER VIII: ADRIAN PLIES HIS HOOK

In the morning, there is much gossip between Raynham and Lobourne involving the fire. Farmer Blaize's property has suffered much; his stables had caught fire, and much of his herd of cattle had perished. Richard and Ripton actually laugh at the event, when they hear of it, as Sir Austin will not admit at this time that he knows what they have done. Instead, he acts "like Providence." He will desire to direct and control events, and it is true that Sir Austin is rather taken aback that his son, the product of such an excellent System, should engage in incendiarism. It should be observed here that what Richard had done, since the fire took place at night, at or near an inhabited dwelling-place, and was set deliberately, was by the law of the times punishable capitally. And Richard, having paid money to have the job done, is equally as guilty as the person who actually set the fire. "In this country, you know, the landlord has always been the pet of the Laws." So Adrian tells the boys; he knows or strongly suspects the situation, and he is having some rather sadistic fun with them. Adrian further tells them that the penalty for rick-burning is at least that of transportation. Very soon, Tom Bakewell is arrested for the crime and locked up in jail to await what the local magistrate will do.

> **Comment: Richard has still not realized what he has done, and only with the suggestions of Adrian as to the serious penalty for rick-burning is he beginning to understand. But there is as yet no remorse, and it is implied that this is the result of the System.**

CHAPTER IX: JUVENILE STRATAGEMS

Richard, as the leader of the duo, suggests to Ripton that the only way to keep their honor is to rescue Tom Bakewell from jail. They purchase a rope and file, hoping to smuggle it to Tom. Richard enlists Austin Wentworth's help, but he flatly refuses: he says to Richard that after he has tried the roundabout method and failed, he, Richard, may come to Austin and learn the straight route. Then Richard, ignoring this, asks Tom Bakewell's mother if she will take the file and rope in when she sees her son in jail.

Adrian, upon learning of all this, laughs - for he professes to see humor in such doings. He is not involved himself; he says that this will be Richard's first brush with experience, and quotes "Diaper Sandoe's" atrociously bad poetry. The final suggestion Adrian has is one which does not face the issue involved in Richard's arson: "Old Blaize will have to be bought off." Austin Wentworth realizes the shallowness of this view, but, even while he senses the trouble building up for Richard, tacitly goes along with the plan.

Comment: The plan to rescue Tom Bakewell involves buying off Farmer Blaize; this is the pragmatic way of doing things suggested by the wise youth, Adrian, who doesn't wish to get involved in the criticism of his patron's System. The dialogue of the chapter is quite indirect and elliptical; it has affinities with the brilliant repartee or wit-combats of Shakespeare. These stylistic features can initially hinder the enjoyment or appreciation of this novel, but one must realize that much of the work is written in a kind of prose-poetry (see the *Essay on Meredith's poetry*, below), and the correct standard to apply is a poetic one.

CHAPTER X: DAPHNE'S BOWER

Austin Wentworth sees Richard, alone, in a secluded temple of white marble nicknamed "Daphne's Bower" by Adrian (Daphne being the laurel tree which the god Apollo had made sacred to his divinity - the novel, incidentally, is filled with such classical references, for purposes we may infer later). Austin Wentworth hears Richard say that Tom Bakewell is a "coward," for not wishing to use the file and rope offered him.

Richard is in a bit of a psychologically vulnerable situation, his friend Ripton having been called back temporarily to London by his father. A Meredithian maxim appears at this point - in explanation of why Austin has such effect on Richard with his argument that Tom is not a coward - but hardly succeeds as such, on top of silence about Richard's part in the arson. "The born preacher we feel instinctively to be our foe.... He may do some good to the wretches that have been struck down, and lie gasping on the battle-field: he rouses deadly antagonism in the strong." The upshot of Austin's advice is that Richard must go down and speak to Farmer Blaize. Richard has, as he says, his pride...but Austin knows just how to appeal to him so that, in the end, he sets off to see Farmer Blaize.

> **Comment: The behavior of Austin Wentworth in this scene, while Meredith does not fall into the trap of dramatically overstating it, is beyond praise. We see that he in truth is one of the stabilizing influences in the strange world of Raynham; he turns, in his interview, Richard's bitter pride into contrition, so that Richard sees that while he may be too proud to go see Farmer Blaize, he still is allowing a young, poor, friendless, and simple boy, Tom Bakewell, to take the punishment which is rightfully Richard's. In this, Austin Wentworth strikes a blow at the effects of the System, which has so far seemed to lead only to selfishness in Richard.**

THE ORDEAL OF RICHARD FEVEREL

TEXTUAL ANALYSIS

CHAPTER 11-20

CHAPTER XI: THE BITTER CUP

When Farmer Blaize is visited by Richard, he seems less surprised to see the young man than might have been expected. In fact, three members of the Feverel family had previously come to see him, separately and secretly: Sir Austin, and then Austin Wentworth, and finally Algernon. Farmer Blaize's terms are hard; he wants three hundred pounds and a spoken apology from Richard. And he will, he says, tolerate no tampering with the Law; in English hearts, "Law was above the sovereign... To tamper with the Law was treason to the realm." Of course, merely by listening to Richard's relatives, he is tampering with the Law, but this is part of Meredith's satiric picture of the honest English yeoman.

The good farmer is still reflecting on whether his three visitors had cooked up their stories, or whether they had come independently, when the fourth arrives, Richard himself. As Richard appears, a fateful meeting very quietly takes place;

a pretty girl of thirteen, the farmer's niece, Lucy Desborough, the orphaned daughter of a Lieutenant of the Royal Navy, is introduced to Richard. At this point, he does not notice her at all, although her uncle introduces her as being a lady, of the family of the Desboroughs of Dorset.

Richard is to swallow the bitter cup of apology to one whom he hates. He tells Farmer Blaize that it was he, Richard, who set fire to the rick. Blaize says that he has come to tell a lie, and asks him to repeat his statement. Richard is still rather haughty, saying that he will pay the full damages if only Blaize will not press charges against poor Tom Bakewell in court the following day, as Tom is very likely to be transported or worse. Blaize is not satisfied, as he tells Richard that he does not like to be lied to. He sends Lucy to fetch someone who is a dependent of the farmer, called The Bantam. "I tell you, young gentleman, the Bantam saw't!"

Comment: Richard is still not doing what he should in the case, and Meredith implies that Blaize's greed for the stiff reimbursement he demands will still not get in the way of his forcing Richard to admit the truth. And this is a part of Richard's education, in defiance of the teachings of the System.

CHAPTER XII: A FINE DISTINCTION

Giles Jinkson is The Bantam; he is a sort of retainer and farm employee of Farmer Blaize, who had been favored over Tom in at least one rather shady transaction by the "honest yeoman," Blaize. The Bantam, upon request from his protector and patron, Blaize, tells Richard what he saw on the night of the fire, speaking in a broad dialect which Meredith is able in his writing to imitate unusually well. The Bantam says that he saw the incident: "A see T'm Baak'll...." He had, he claims, seen Tom set the fire. Richard claims that he himself had set the fire, and Bakewell was innocent. This staggers The Bantam, who had apparently been bribed to say that Bakewell did it by certain pieces of gold given him by persons not mentioned.

Hearing Richard tell a different story, The Bantam starts to become vague and confused in his own story. This enrages Blaize, who believes that his best witness against Tom has been tampered with, which indeed he has been. He says that Tom Bakewell must travel (transportation, the usual penalty for such an agricultural outrage being a sentence of perhaps seven years - to be transported to a penal colony, such as Botany Bay, in Australia, Jamaica, or, also off Australia, Norfolk Island, or Tasmania. In the case of Tom Bakewell, Farmer Blaize is making a real enough threat.) This reaction is in part chagrin at his witness being tampered with; it also stems in part from the wish of the agricultural yeoman or small farmer to get back at "the gentry," while at the same time maintaining respectful deference to his "betters." There is now the possibility of serious trouble for Richard as a result of this **episode**. How will he, as well as Tom Bakewell, be rescued?

> **Comment: A point to note in this chapter is the ambivalent attitude toward the gentry of such a person as Farmer Blaize. He respects them profoundly, and addresses Richard as "young gentleman," while at the same time insisting that he, Blaize, is as good as the gentry are. He also respects Richard for having "a conscience about a poor man," that is, Tom Bakewell. These attitudes, irrational and self-contradictory as they may be, are typical of the age and locale - and we have seen from Meredith's**

biography just why he was so fascinated by the concept of the English Gentleman, trained to lead the Farmer Blaizes, Tom Bakewells, Ripton Thompsons, and Bantams of this world.

CHAPTER XIII: RICHARD PASSES THROUGH HIS PRELIMINARY ORDEAL, AND IS THE OCCASION OF AN APHORISM

As Richard returns to Raynham Abbey after his highly unsuccessful interview with Farmer Blaize, he sees, by accident, the book of Sir Austin's Aphorisms open on the bedroom dressing-table. And the aphorism which is in full view is:

> "The Dog returneth to his Vomit; the Liar must eat his Lie."

And underneath, in pencil, the bare statement: "The Devil's mouthful."

Richard goes to dinner, feeling somehow as if his father had struck him in the face. But after dinner, father and son retire, and simply sit in each other's company for an hour, with no word spoken. Later, the fact of the visits to Farmer Blaize by the members of the family, each unknown to the other, comes out. Sir Austin resolves to go again to Farmer Blaize and speak with him, pledging that there had been no tampering with witnesses. But Adrian tells Richard that Sir Austin ought not to swear to such a thing; he does not say why, but Richard understands the unspoken message well enough, and stops his father, asking that he, Richard, as is his place since he was responsible for the rick-burning, be allowed to go himself. As the chapter concludes, Richard is heading toward a second meeting with Blaize, while Sir Austin is congratulating himself that all is well:

"There is for the mind but one grasp of Happiness: from that uppermost pinnacle of Wisdom, whence we see that this world is well-designed." So he writes in his notebook of aphorisms. In view of the tragic ending to which his own course of conduct will lead, this is an ironic statement.

> **Comment:** In this chapter, there is almost a dialectic among the various characters, again half-comic, on the nature of Truth and the difficulties to which lying can bring one. Richard has to find this out for himself; he cannot be given ready-made defenses against life by the System, as Sir Austin seems to believe. Unfortunately, it is Sir Austin who fails to learn what he should from this episode; it is somehow ethically disreputable, the way Sir Austin has handled the situation. Richard is learning, but Sir Austin's invincible self-conviction that his System is correct has not weakened; it has rather been strengthened. The penning of the aphorism at the end has a sinister note, because it proves that Sir Austin has learned nothing from the Farmer Blaize episode.

CHAPTER XIV: IN WHICH THE LAST ACT OF THE BAKEWELL COMEDY IS CLOSED IN A LETTER

Back home in London, Ripton Thompson is very much disturbed. He is, in a double sense, "under the roofs of Law." His father is, of course, a lawyer; but more than this, Ripton is temporarily away from the indirect influence of the System, which as Meredith treats it is not Law, but its opposite Arson is revealed to Ripton now in terms of all of its awful legal penalties. He is very disturbed, then, as even members of his family note, though they have no knowledge of the reason, until Letitia Thompson, "Miss Letty," Ripton's sister, discovers a letter Richard had written his friend concerning the outcome of the proceedings against Tom Bakewell, which had led to a sudden change in Ripton's spirits from depression to joy Now Miss Letty knows what has been going on, and she returns the letter, after three readings of it, to Ripton's jacket, as Richard had written under a charge of very strict secrecy, already violated by Ripton's careless handling of the letter.

The letter indicates that Tom Bakewell had been let off, after Richard had spoken to Farmer Blaize and humbled himself. Also, there was confirmation of the fact that Adrian had bribed The Bantam to change his testimony, so that Tom Bakewell was freed by the magistrate for lack of evidence - and the said magistrate, Sir Miles Papworth, was very hard on people accused of rickburning and would have been likely to give Tom the maximum penalty. But Tom's "alibi" had been established by a discrepancy in the times which were involved in the case; for at nine o'clock in the evening in question, Tom was seen drinking in the ale-house at Bursley with the Tinker, and The Bantam had said that he saw someone, whom he thought was Tom, at that same hour by the rick which was burned.

Meredith's dryly ironic last sentence of this chapter is this: "And so ended the last act of the *Bakewell Comedy*, on which the curtain closes with Sir Austin's pointing out to his friends the beneficial action of the System in it from beginning to end.

Comment: The story is still ambiguous, and with the ending of this chapter, we have the ending of a major section of the novel; the first third, which has established the characterization of most of the

principals and has also indicated the pernicious effects of the System. The point is that Sir Austin is just as convinced as ever that his System is correct and, indeed, that in the case of the rick-burning episode, the System had worked perfectly.

CHAPTER XV: THE BLOSSOMING SEASON

In this long chapter, Richard grows into young manhood, still under the influence of the System. He has had one brief exposure to the world, in the matter of Farmer Blaize. Ripton has not been invited back permanently to be with Richard, as Sir Austin felt that his son had learned quite enough from the experience, which he blamed in some degree on Ripton, although, actually Richard was from first to last the ringleader. To replace Ripton, Richard has Tom Bakewell, who serves him and whom he attempts to teach letters, military bearing, and even prayer.

Sir Austin calls this time between simple boyhood and adolescence, "The Blossoming Season," in which the boy is unselfish. But this doctrinaire observation, which he writes down in his notebook, is still a fraudulent observation, because Sir Austin is attributing Richard's development to the success of the System, whereas the reverse is the truth: he is developing surprisingly well, despite the System. Lady Blandish reads Sir Austin's aphorisms from *The Pilgrim's Scrip* to Richard, and he professes to understand them and to believe her (which he does) when she tells him that his father is very wise. Richard goes through various youthful phases: he is attracted to such fads as vegetarianism; he is temporarily religious, but this too is a phase; he attempts to teach Tom Bakewell. Finally, he begins to write poetry, then he unexpectedly burns all of his manuscript poems, and he does this at the suggestion, but not at the command, of Sir Austin. And, as Meredith says in conclusion of this chapter, with the burning of the manuscripts, the possibility of "true confidence" between father and son evaporates.

> **Comment: This chapter covers quite a bit of time, chronologically. Richard develops into a physically healthy and active boy. Still, he is being tampered with psychologically by his father's System, and the rick-burning incident, which should have opened Sir Austin's eyes to the faults of the System, only close them further and leave him blind to the ill he is doing to his son.**

CHAPTER XVI: THE MAGNETIC AGE

This is the Age of violent attractions between persons of opposite sex, and Sir Austin is trying to guard against the possibility that Richard will see or hear something which, to put the situation crudely, will arouse him before Sir Austin wishes him to become interested in such things. Therefore, the baronet tells Adrian that whatever goes on at Raynham, as among the servants, it must and will be handled discreetly. Adrian's tuition is "able"; he is interested in the more attractive of the servant girls, but indeed he is discreet. To make certain of Richard's security, Sir Austin exiles Clare, because he feels that Richard might notice her - but Mrs. Doria Forey is indignant and has several reasons, one of them, as we have noted, being that she intends that Clare marry Richard.

Meanwhile, Lady Blandish has been working on Sir Austin, praising the effect of his System on Richard - and as yet "it could not be said that Sir Austin's System had failed. On the contrary, it had reared a youth handsome, intelligent, well-bred, and, observed the ladies, with acute emphasis, innocent." This pleases Sir Austin, who, in speaking to Lady Blandish of

Richard, attacks the double standard and insists that his System is designed to hold men to the same high moral standards as women are held to in his society - although he does not put the case in quite these terms.

Lady Blandish seems to expect that Sir Austin will propose to her, and is taken aback when Sir Austin instead asks her about the marriage of Richard He is now almost eighteen, and Sir Austin intends that he shall marry when he is about twenty-five. And Sir Austin already visualizes the kind of girl whom Richard will marry: preferably a few years younger than Richard, an only child, and not necessarily wealthy or of aristocratic heritage. If she comes of good stock, she will serve. At the conclusion of the chapter, Lady Blandish has attained the honor of being allowed to hold Sir Austin's hand - but unfortunately for her, he does not propose marriage, then or later, and she is living in a vain expectation.

Comment: Under the humorous social comedy of the consultation with Lady Blandish and with-his sister, Mrs. Forey, over Richard's possible marriage, there is a good bit of lightly-handled but serious social comment in this chapter. As is wellknown, the adjective Victorian signifies stuffiness, prudery, too-great reticence about the primary human relation: that between the sexes. This Victorianism was largely confined to the middle and upper classes in England, and part of it is perceived today to be sheer myth. But still, in Victorian middle- and upper-class England, women were placed on a pedestal, and to them was attributed purity and complete innocence, especially of the fact of human sexuality. Men were thought to be somehow "lower" creatures in this respect, and thus the maintenance of Richard's

innocence, as the quality which Sir Austin was trying to foster in him was often called, is proportionately more remarkable because its absence from most boys of his age, or so Sir Austin wishes to believe.

There is actually an intense sexual awareness in a chapter of this tone, though Meredith does well in disguising his subject. It must be remembered that the "Ordeal" which Richard undergoes is formally the "Ordeal of Women," but actually it is that of his father's System. The relation of Richard to various woman, as well as to his father, is what the novel is "about," at least on one level of interpretation. *The Ordeal of Richard Feverel*, read through modern eyes, seems tame enough. But when it was published, it shocked many. Magnetism, in this chapter, is a synonym for sexual attraction and it was part of the formal mores of the times that such attraction either did not exist, or, if people recognized the fact which was only too apparent, that it was something low and to be kept in strict bounds, as Sir Austin attempts to do with his System.

The above is quite oversimplified, but it should be kept in mind that for this novel to have been published in 1859, in the heart of the mid-Victorian age, is remarkable from this point of view alone, even if there were not artistic factors involved that make it one of the great English works of fiction of the century. Meredith never descends to the gross, but in his scenes involving romantic love and one of its primary components, sexual attraction or magnetism - the phrases here are as stuffy and pompous as many of Meredith's contemporaries were on these matters - Meredith is exceptionally frank, although within the boundaries allowed him by his age. *The Ordeal of Richard Feverel* is, as this chapter begins to establish, a novel of sexual modernism - but the modernism of 1859, in a special social stratum of Victorian England; it has affinities with, but is in no sense the same as, the modernism of, say, D. H. Lawrence, though in the subscription to the doctrine of what we have here described as Vitalism, these two authors did have something in common.

CHAPTER XVII: AN ATTRACTION

This is a continuation of the preceding chapter, in that Richard is becoming interested in women. When Meredith writes, by way of circumlocution, "All night Richard tossed on his bed with his heart in a rapid canter, and his brain bestriding it, traversing the rich untasted world, and the great Realm of Mystery, from which he was now restrained no longer...," this is a way of saying that Richard is in the grip of the desire for romance and the fact of sexuality. He wishes to write more poetry, but Sir Austin has "shut that safety-valve." Richard leaves the house very early in the morning, and meets his young Etonian friend, Ralph Morton, who is joining the Army. Young Morton gets from Richard, on a thin pretext, the address of Clare Forey. Meanwhile, Richard moves further into the Mystery he is pursuing when he sees a "daughter of Earth," a young girl, by a lake, eating dewberries. "When Nature has made us ripe for Love it seldom occurs that the Fates are behindhand in furnishing a Temple for the flame." This epigram is not Sir Austin's, but that of Meredith himself, and one can see which way the action of the chapter is tending.

Comment: In this chapter, Richard meets the girl who is to be his fate. While Meredith skillfully avoids direct statement of the fact, it is clear that a combination of Richard's very romantic imagination and his physical desires have combined to lead him to this meeting with the girl whom, although he does not know it, he already had met some five years previously.

CHAPTER XVIII: FERDINAND AND MIRANDA

This famous chapter chronicles, in poetic language, the meeting of Richard Feverel and Lucy Desborough. They had met before, as Lucy had been Richard's defender in the household of Farmer Blaize - but that was years earlier, when they were children. Now they are not children. She is the "First Woman" to him; he is a prince, to her.

The scene is modeled, by design, very closely on Shakespeare's grave and romantic philosophical comedy, *The Tempest*. The best of Meredith, indeed, often has a Shakespearean ring to it, but Meredith keeps this from being too derivative. Ferdinand is the King's son in *The Tempest*, who marries the daughter of the philosopher and wonder-worker, the Duke Prospero. In winning the girl, Miranda, Ferdinand is tested by Prospero by the performance of menial tasks. And here, in this crucial chapter of *The Ordeal*, a new Ferdinand meets his Miranda.

Furthermore, Lucy had been following Richard from afar for years, and just by coincidence he finds her reading some fragment of his verses, which she had gotten in some strange way or another. She tells Richard that she was at Belthorpe, "old Blaize's farm," when they first met, and that she is Farmer

Blaize's niece. He remembers the Desboroughs of Dorset, and especially does he remember Lucy. As the scene closes, he succumbs to instinct, telling her that she is his love. "Perfect simplicity is unconsciously audacious," comments Meredith on Richard's declaration. Just as Ferdinand and Miranda fall instantly in love with each other on first meeting, so do Richard and Lucy. But, as Meredith adds in a more sinister vein, Sir Austin is not a Prospero.

> **Comment: Here is a scene of love at first sight, an "elective affinity," in Browning's sense. This in itself is rather daringly handled by Meredith in this crucial scene. His point is that Nature speaks, and these two children of Nature, who have not yet been corrupted by any System or false teaching, heed the voice. In contrast to Prospero, whose wide guidance, amounting to the superhuman, insures the successful ending in the play of the marriage of Ferdinand and Miranda - the reconciliation of opposites, and the pardoning of enemies-Sir Austin can do none of these, although he probably fancies himself to be a Prospero. He is, but it is a Prospero turned backwards. (The author's Bright Note Study Guide to *The Tempest*, especially the characterizations of Prospero, Ferdinand, and Miranda, p. 62 ff., may be of interest to present readers - Editor's note.)**

CHAPTER XIX: UNMASKING OF MASTER RIPTON THOMPSON

Sir Austin is meanwhile going about finding the girl whom Richard should marry by a scientific search; he actually has a notebook in which are listed suitable families, each designated by what they have to recommend them: Money (M.), Position (Po.), or Principles, (Pr.), as he abbreviates these. The baronet is visiting his lawyer. After some business discussion, the two men turn to a discussion of what is at the moment closer to their minds, their sons and heirs, Richard and Ripton.

A very comical scene with serious undertones now ensues, treated with great sophistication by Meredith. It involves Ripton, whose character and outlook on life we already have some occasion to know. Sir Austin first begins to explain his System to Mr. Thompson. The lawyer is a good enough businessman not to contradict one of his most important and most wealthy clients, who is a personal friend as well. But to him, Sir Austin is talking utter nonsense - and Meredith, of course, shares this view, as his satiric picture of Sir Austin shows. He "elaborated his theory of Organism and Mechanism, for his lawyer's edification." But Mr. Thompson simply says that he agrees, and, unfortunately, chooses this time to ring for Ripton Thompson, whom they will examine to see how his own upbringing is affecting him. Unfortunately, because the result of this incident, ironically, confirms Sir Austin in all of his beliefs about the System.

Comment: This scene is very sophisticated, and it concerns the different views of Ripton held by his father and by Sir Austin, the latter taking heart about the effectiveness of the System from seeing the kind of mildly dissolute life which Ripton, outwardly a repressed and proper Victorian youngman, is leading. What he has in his desk, and what he has been reading, instead of the law of Gavelkind (an obscure point of the law of land inheritance, peculiar to the county of Kent, in England - where the land goes simultaneously to more than one son of a family, unlike the practice in most common-law

areas). He has been reading what might be called low illustrated magazines, not exactly pornographic, for example, The Adventures of Miss Random, its title sufficiently suggestive of its contents.

Ripton has embarrassed his father no end with such red-handed discovery in front of his powerful patron and friend. But the effect on Sir Austin is pernicious, because, as stated, it makes him even more sure that the repressive System will result in a better future for Richard, in terms of his moral and spiritual health, than could the random upbringing of a Ripton Thompson will have. Actually, the result will be precisely the opposite, as we will see.

CHAPTER XX: GOOD WINE AND GOOD BLOOD

Sir Austin and his solicitor have an extensive discussion about Ripton's reading matter, and Sir Austin self-confidently says that the expected nothing more, in view of the kind of upbringing that most young men have. Ripton's father is very much embarrassed and wonders if Ripton will ever again be invited to Raynham. Of course he will be invited, says Sir Austin. Meanwhile, he gives Ripton's father advice on how to bring him up so that he will not trifle with vice. In fact, Sir Austin suggests that Ripton be allowed to see the very worst "sinks" of town, so that he will become disgusted with vice. "What home is pure absolutely? What cannot our doctors and lawyers tell us?" says Richard's father.

The lawyer's answer is to have a glass of excellent Port wine, and to launch into a speech on the deterioration of the vintage. What Sir Austin had been talking about was the deterioration of the race through the vices caused by undisciplined sexual desire - since this novel, is, after all, written in mid-Victorian England, the actual import of what Sir Austin says about the sins of the fathers being visited on the sons is quite disguised. To be blunt, he is talking about the ruination of families through venereal disease. These illnesses, it should be remembered by those even minimally acquainted with medical history, were simply not curable until discoveries made by Dr. Paul Ehrlich and others, about 1900. Now, this is an idea that in no way is stated directly in *The Ordeal of Richard Feverel*, but it is implied on every page, and certainly is implicit in the motivation of Sir Austin's System.

> **Comment: The double standard of sexual morality, which meant that there was one standard, a secretly rather permissive one, for men, and a much higher standard of chastity and "purity" for women, obtained in the English Victorian middle and upper classes, as is well known. Women were regarded with worship, so long as they retained their chastity or were lawfully married. However, a woman, once "fallen," as the phrase was, had little to look forward to except death or the poorhouse. Men, while formally held to the same strict standard, actually were able to "sow their wild oats," as the euphemism was at the time. A young man, especially, such as Ripton Thompson, could be expected to do exactly what he evidently has been doing (if one reads this chapter very carefully). The great danger in such activity, according to the standards of society, apart from the moral decay involved, was the distinct possibility of venereal infection which, as stated, could be arrested but could never be cured**

before the twentieth century. And such infection could be transmitted within a family, visited on innocent children. Sir Austin's point is that with his strict repressive upbringing of Richard by means of the System, such corruption simply could not enter into the Feverel family. Whether he is right will be seen later.

THE ORDEAL OF RICHARD FEVEREL

TEXTUAL ANALYSIS

CHAPTER 21-30

CHAPTER XXI: THE SYSTEM ENCOUNTERS THE WILD OATS SPECIAL PLEA

This chapter extends the implied points made in the preceding, especially on the subject of the sowing of wild oats. It, too, as is evident from the very title of the chapter, discusses at a rather sophisticated level the question of the worth of letting young men engage in excesses of behavior before they marry or settle down. The "special plea" is advanced to Sir Austin by two of his friends; Lord Heddon, and Darley Absworthy, his distant cousin also - both influential men who are also members of Parliament.

Briefly, the argument they use is an ancient and worldly one. Lord Heddon states it to Sir Austin, and it is that a lad should experiment with vice so that he will know virtue. "You can't expect to have a man, if he doesn't take a man's food. You'll have a milksop." This argument is of course politely rejected by Sir Austin, who feels that in bringing Richard up repressively, according to his System, he is preventing the kind of disaster or biological weakening of the stock of a family which he sees occurring in other people and their children and grandchildren. "This universal ignorance of the inevitable consequence of Sin is frightful! The Wild Oats plea is a torpedo that seems to have struck the world, and rendered it morally insensible." So observes Sir Austin, as he calls into question the wild oats theory of behavior, if we can dignify it with such a name.

Comment: Sir Austin is actually in London to find a fit wife for Richard, and the word gets around so that many visiting-cards are left him by mothers of families of suitable social station. Sir Austin, with his theory that many if not most families have been corrupted by Wild Oats and the double standard, is suspicious of most possibilities for his son. He takes the occasion, as he had with Ripton Thompson's father, to more or less gloat over his righteousness in his System of bringing up Richard.

Paradoxically, while Sir Austin is wrong, in Meredith's satiric view, in the ways he is employing to bring up Richard, according a System whose chief defects are its inflexibility and its disregard of Nature, he is at the same time right in many of his observations about the current state of affairs regarding the upbringing of children of the middle and upper classes in Victorian England. He is thus, simultaneously, a satiric and an anti-satiric character, and this is a very sophisticated presentation of him on Meredith's part. Sir Austin is right about his final objective, but wrong, about the means which he uses to attain it - and the reason he is wrong in Meredith's view, is that he forgets that Richard is a sovereign

personality and treats him as an instrument, to prove something, namely, Sir Austin's own rightness.

CHAPTER XXII: A SHADOWY VIEW OF COELEBS PATER GOING ABOUT WITH A GLASS-SLIPPER

This is a scintillating chapter of social comedy, involving the design of a Mrs. Caroline Grandison, a widow with eight daughters, who is hoping to marry one of her daughters to Richard. She professed to understand Sir Austin's System well. The symbol of the Glass Slipper here refers, of course, to the slipper in the Cinderella fairytale...many of the girls in London trying on the slipper, which in this context is a **metaphor** for their becoming the choice of Sir Austin as Richard's bride.

Sir Miles Papworth had arranged the introduction of Mrs. Grandison to Sir Austin, mentioning to her that Feverel had an income of fifty thousand a year. Now, this was really a tremendous fortune in those times, and allowing for considerable exaggeration, should certainly have attracted marriage prospects to Richard. By the end of this long chapter, though, it appears that Mrs. Grandison has the inside track in her pursuit of Richard. There is a paragraph hidden in the chapter, however, which implies that Richard is otherwise occupying himself. "There was a damsel closer home...." This refers to the same Lucy Desborough, niece of Farmer Blaize, whom Richard had met twice before. The contrast between the actuality of Richard's interests and the doctrinaire notions of Sir Austin is part of the meaning of an otherwise rather diffuse chapter.

Comment: The chapter may seem relatively tedious, and after all, Mrs. Grandison is herself tedious with

her transparent scheme to snare Richard and his inheritance. But this is the point: Sir Austin is taken in. All he requires is a bit of not-so-subtle flattery on the part of prospective daughter-in-law's scheming mother, a bit of praise of his System, and he is capable of being hoodwinked - which would not be so bad, except that it is Richard's happiness with which he is trifling.

CHAPTER XXIII: A DIVERSION PLAYED ON A PENNY-WHISTLE

As the preceding chapter is satirical, almost tediously so because of the boring nature of the moralizing on both sides, so this chapter is its opposite - poetic and lyrical. "Away with Systems! Away with a corrupt World! Let us breathe the air of the Enchanted Island!" So Meredith begins this section, with another reference to the "enchanted island" of Shakespeare's play, The Tempest, with the analogy to the meeting of Ferdinand and Miranda. Its concern is entirely with love; the love-affair of Richard and Lucy. The work, further, because of the superb nature of its poetic **imagery** and lyrical handling of the subject, speaks for itself. It is a prose-poem which must be appreciated in the light of Meredith's high achievement, at his best, as a poet. It can be said that at this point occurs the demise of Sir Austin's System, under the promptings of unperverted nature. This chapter is one of the great achievements of *The Ordeal of Richard Feverel*, and should be viewed from that perspective.

> **Comment: Though the section above seems lyrical and uninformed by much thought, Meredith has a distinct intellectual purpose in writing it. In his trinity of blood, brain, and spirit, it is the first out of which the other two rise - and Sir Austin would**

defy the teachings of Nature. In this scene, Nature asserts herself and her rights, showing exactly how shallow and selfish was the theory of Richard's father in seeking to interfere with the life-renewing commands of Nature and in attempting to bypass blood in favor of brain - we shall see presently how this idea is further developed.

CHAPTER XXIV: CELEBRATES THE TIME-HONORED TREATMENT OF A DRAGON BY THE HERO

In the preceding chapter, the action of the story is very quickly advanced - Richard's falling in love with Lucy and the mutual acknowledgment of that love signals the death of Sir Austin's System, although its evil effects may remain. Here Sir Austin writes his adviser Adrian about Mrs. Grandison and the possibility that one of her daughters will be selected for Richard's wife. Meanwhile, a Miss Molly Davenport, one of the girls working on the farm, informs Adrian where Richard is. He is with Farmer Blaize's niece, she says, after accepting a present of money from Adrian. They are innocent, she adds. The reason Lucy has not been seen at Church by Adrian is that she is a Roman Catholic, as was her father - she had gone to school to be taught by nuns for three years, and has a small inheritance of her own. Adrian succeeds in worming all the information available out of Molly. But he chooses not to say anything about the Lucy **episode** to Sir Austin at this time, because "It's the Inevitable," he thinks - and he has no faith in the System.

Meanwhile Heavy Benson also has knowledge of the affair of Richard and Lucy, and as he is a rival for Sir Austin's favor with Adrian, he determines that he can do something to prove his greater loyalty to his chief. Tom Bakewell gets wind of the spying which

Benson is doing on Richard, and tells Richard of this. Benson writes a letter warning Sir Austin, in London, of the affair. Lady Blandish has also seen Lucy, and admires her very much - what a pity, she adds to Adrian, that Lucy isn't of the proper social class for Richard. "How absurd it is of that class to educate their women above their station!"

Lady Blandish and Adrian overhear Lucy and Richard; Heavy Benson also hears. Richard catches Benson spying, and beats him up, because he also knows that it is Benson who has written to Sir Austin. As the chapter ends, the Lucy-Richard relationship has certainly been discovered by all concerned in the family, as the result of the joint spying of Benson, Adrian, and Lady Blandish.

Comment: The question of Lucy's Catholic religion is a relatively clumsy artistic device, raised at this point by Meredith to explain the coming opposition of Sir Austin to her as Richard's possible wife. There was little likelihood of a girl of Lucy's background being other than a Protestant in rural England of the nineteenth century, and, as a matter of fact, Roman Catholics were not permitted to vote or to sit in the English Parliament until 1829. It may be seen that on religious grounds alone Richard's father would be opposed to such a marriage, for there would be in the countryside something of a stigma attached to Lucy. Added to the prejudice resulting from religious difference is the prejudice of class; Richard, especially in view of his potentially great financial prospects as the heir of Sir Austin and the chief of the Feverel family, would be marrying "beneath" himself if he were to marry Lucy. But all of these objections, while they justify Sir Austin in his own eyes, do not explain fully his objections. He objects simply because

Richard has gone against him and has demonstrated a will of his own, despite the System.

However, the difference in religion is one explanation of the relative ease with which Sir Austin convinces Richard to live apart from his wife, later, after they are married and even while Lucy is pregnant with Richard's child. It would hardly be believable otherwise that Richard should act in this manner, but Meredith tries to make his reasons for the separation convincing, as we shall see. The spying with which Richard is surrounded helps to prove the basic bankruptcy of Sir Austin's System, for if Sir Austin really believed in the capability of the System, he would have more trust in Richard.

CHAPTER XXV: RICHARD IS SUMMONED TO TOWN TO HEAR A SERMON

Berry, the Baronet's personal servant, arrives in haste from London with strict orders to bring Richard back with him. Incidentally, Berry is one of the comic characters in the novel, along with The Bantam and Tom Bakewell; the humor in Berry's case comes from his wild misuse of the English language. Adrian finds a way to talk Richard around, by means of a lying trick - but Adrian's philosophy in this as in other matters in distinctly that the end justifies the means. For, evidently, he has told Richard that his father wishes to see him because he, Sir Austin, is quite ill with apoplexy. Richard instantly rushes on horseback to London.

Once there, he sees that his father is not ill, and is somewhat puzzled. But his father quotes a maxim which leads Richard to know that "he knows all," that is, all about Lucy, whom Richard had promised to meet that same night. He wishes to leave for the railway station, so that he may return to Raynham in time to meet Lucy. Of course he does not tell his purpose to his father. But the Baronet stops him with a gesture and begins to deliver a "sermon." The essence of the sermon is this: "There are women in the world, my son!" He adds that women represent the Ordeal of the Feverels. And his argument sways Richard, until Sir Austin is foolish enough to say too much, and speak of young men who fancy that they may be in love, ruining their lives through a rash marriage. Richard hears, but at this point he ceases to listen. His father asks if Richard has anything to tell him. "I have not." Richard's answer provokes Sir Austin's wish that he remain in town that night, and then Richard realizes that he has been told an untruth: his father is not ill.

> **Comment: Here we can see the dawning of real mutual distrust between father and son, amid an atmosphere of spying and deception. Richard has been lured to London on a pretext, and this kind of behavior on the part of those who deceived him is likely to insure that he will not trust them again.**

CHAPTER XXVI: INDICATES THE APPROACHES OF FEVER

Richard is confined, so to speak, in London for three weeks, while listening to the teachings of the System. Sir Austin introduces him to the daughters of Mrs. Grandison - at the same time he has Richard taken on carefully-supervised but passive tours of the London red-light district, though the latter is merely hinted at in Meredith's oblique way. Carola, Mrs. Grandison's daughter, comes to know Richard, and confides in him that what she would really like to be is a boy. At this, he confides in her.

Meanwhile, Adrian writes to the baronet that "the young person has resigned the neighborhood." He has induced Lucy to leave. For one thing, Farmer Blaize intends that she shall marry his own son, Tom, and one can assume that with the sturdy independence of the British Yeomanry, Farmer Blaize does not wish his ward Lucy to become involved with Richard, so far above her in social class. "God bless the Squire and his relations, and keep us in our proper Stations...." So runs the jingle of the proper relationships among the classes in the England of the centuries before the First World War.

Lady Blandish has also written to Sir Austin. She, too, has spoken privately to Lucy. The appeal which Lady Blandish has made is in a way a dishonorable one: she has asked Lucy to give up Richard for his own sake. Also, Lady Blandish supposes that she will be able to enlist Sir Austin's aid in preventing Lucy's marriage to Farmer Blaize's "lout of a son," as she is much too good for him.

Lady Blandish gets in a few words on behalf of her own subtle designs on Sir Austin; she praises some of his maxims in The Pilgrim's Scrip, but his mood is such that he is far from flattered. Meanwhile, Richard returns to Raynham and, meeting Tom Bakewell, learns that Lucy is gone. He is outwardly calm, but inwardly raging; he determines to follow her instantly, but the question is: where have they taken her? He does not know, nor does Tom.

Comment: Sir Austin's arbitrary and indeed despicable action here will turn Richard permanently against him. Further, it is a self-defeating action because, instead of weakening Lucy's attractiveness for Richard, it vastly increases it.

Some of the conversation in this chapter is extremely subtle, especially that between Carola and Richard, and if one accepts uncritically the Freudian interpretation of literature, one can find much Freudian material in Carola's expressed wish to be a boy and to be permitted not to ride side-saddle. But whether Meredith had in mind these Freudian classical notions of sexual envy and rivalry is highly debatable, and it may be lacking in sense of humor even to suggest this. The point is that, writing three or four decades before Freud's pioneering work had begun even being thought of, Meredith was intuitively treating the subject of a well-adjusted approach to the fact of human sexuality in a most modern way, and this in defiance of Victorian conventionalism. And this is the explanation and the justification for much of the indirection and elliptical language used by Meredith in this novel.

CHAPTER XXVII: CRISIS IN THE APPLE-DISEASE

Richard visits the home of Farmer Blaize at night, and is invited in; he wishes to see where his beloved Lucy had lived, although immediately upon entering the house he can feel, by its deadness, that she is no longer there. They have an extensive discussion, during which Richard pleads with Blaize to bring Lucy back, for he promises to marry her the day he is of age. Blaize respects the young man more now, but can only say that she will be away until the spring; that he had given his word to certain people. Richard realizes who those certain people are, and he is beside himself. On the way back he travels in the rain, and falls senseless, and evidently seriously ill, in the Inn on the way back to Raynham. Sir Austin believes that when Richard recovers from his "fever," he will be cured of his love for Lucy - so the System teaches.

> Comment: This scene, in its long confrontation between Richard and Farmer Blaize, provides additional exposition, and shows the development of Richard's character. He acts like a man, not a boy, in his honest discussion with Blaize. Meredith's preoccupation with social station is satisfied as we learn more of Lucy's background - the family are gentlefolk from way back, and her father had, as we know, been a Lieutenant in the Royal Navy and thus, ex officio and by act of King and Parliament, a Gentleman. This is important to show her suitability for Richard. At the end, Sir Austin shows his cold heartlessness in rather rejoicing that his son is ill so that he will be cured of the "fever" (cf. the suggestion of the name itself, Feverel) of the Apple-Disease.

CHAPTER XXVIII: OF THE SPRING PRIMROSE AND THE AUTUMNAL

Richard, as he recovers slowly from his illness, seems to have in truth lost interest in Lucy, even as Sir Austin had predicted. Richard is almost too good, in the eyes of the Baronet, even of Heavy Benson, in his "reformation." Tom Bakewell has said that he was ordered by his young master never to mention the name of Lucy to him as long as he lived, so the elders of Raynham are convinced that Richard is not playing a part. Lady Blandish is impressed by Sir Austin's "wisdom," rather in spite of herself, for she is disturbed that love could be so quickly quenched by parental disapproval. Lady Blandish has sentimental feelings toward Sir Austin. Now, one of the key quotations from The

Pilgrim's Scrip is interjected here: "Sentimentalists are they who seek to enjoy Reality, without incurring the Immense Debtorship for a thing done." But Sir Austin, while he enjoys the company of Lady Blandish, goes no further, for he has the memory of the woman who had deserted him, and he is still legally her husband, we must assume. This chapter seems to discuss Lady Blandish and her plans more than Richard, but Richard is still present, in his apparent indifference to Lucy and his vindication, for the time being, of the System.

> **Comment:** The quotation concerning sentimentalism is one of the key such aphorisms in the book. It was used by Joyce at an important point in his masterpiece, *Ulysses*. Its use here in *The Ordeal of Richard Feverel*, however, is both "straight" and ironic - it is spoken, or written, by Sir Austin, but if he only realized the implications of the statement, he would apply it first of all to himself. Elsewhere, Meredith says of sentimentalists that they "fiddle harmonics on the strings of sensualism," and this oblique saying, with allowances made for the Meredithian avoidance of strict Victorian mores, means that basically the sentimentalist, however he disguises his feelings under fine notions of self-sacrifice, perverts and deceives himself as to the end of Nature's great plan for the continuance and further development of the race.

CHAPTER XXIX: IN WHICH THE HERO TAKES A STEP

Sir Austin is apprehensive about Richard's manner, now that he is in better health and it is spring. He seems frozen, and he will not take anyone into his confidence. But neither will he even mention Lucy. The baronet decides that Richard needs some distractions, which the City, London, can provide. Richard plans to go to visit the Grandisons, especially Carola, with his father's approval. Richard seems restrained, dignified, even grave, but as he is in his seat on the train which is to carry him to London with Tom Bakewell, Sir Austin observes him to burst out laughing. Richard quotes many verses of Diaper Sandoe to his uncle, Hippias Feverel, who doesn't know what to make of the conversation. Meanwhile, Tom Bakewell has seen Tom Blaize all dressed up, on the same train heading for London, to pick up someone...and of course the someone is Lucy. Richard can now find out where she is. Richard instantly realizes that they had known at Raynham of Lucy's return, and therefore had sent him to London to get him out of the way again. But now he is tougher, and he lays his plans.

Comment: Richard, having been lied to once by his father and other relatives in the matter of Lucy's whereabouts, is determined not to allow himself to be taken in again. This time, he has made elaborate and hidden plans; he even knows which railway line Lucy would have to take to return to Raynham. And he will be waiting.

CHAPTER XXX: RECORDS THE RAPID DEVELOPMENT OF THE HERO

Ripton Thompson, now at work in his father's legal office in London, suddenly receives a mysterious note: "You are to get lodgings for a lady immediately. Not a word to a soul...." It is signed with the initials of his friend, R.D.F.

Ripton, unable to find out more from Tom Bakewell, who has delivered the note, accompanies him, after having engaged rooms from a Mrs. Elizabeth Berry, a landlady in Kensington.

Ripton then goes to Richard at a hotel in Westminster. Richard escorts down a young lady, her face hidden by a veil. It is, of course, Lucy, whom Ripton at this time scarcely knows. Richard is evidently going to defy his family and to marry the girl; Ripton, for his bumbling pseudo-sophistication, can see that the matter involves marriage and not another kind of relationship.

Richard presently tells Ripton the story of what he is planning to do, and why. "They've been plotting against me for a year," he says. Richard has concluded that, having located Lucy by a lucky accident, which "must have been Fate," he will marry her. If his father really cares for him, he will forgive this elopement. Richard and Ripton return to the vicinity of Mrs. Berry's house, where Lucy is staying, but they are so excited at the plan Richard has that they have actually forgotten where the house is...but eventually they find it.

Comment: Perhaps Meredith uses a bit too much coincidence in this chapter. But this is not a serious artistic defect, because after all Richard was being sent to London to get him out of the way for Lucy's return; so it follows that he has a chance of intercepting her, especially after he recognizes Tom Blaize heading in the same direction. With Richard's open defiance of his training and of the System, we see its final invalidation. He also behaves, naturally and without the necessity of any System, as a perfect gentleman toward Lucy, who has put herself, as a bad Victorian play might say, completely in his power. If his intentions toward her did not involve honorable marriage, she would be defenseless.

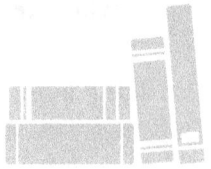

THE ORDEAL OF RICHARD FEVEREL

TEXTUAL ANALYSIS

CHAPTERS 31-40

CHAPTER XXXI: CONTAINS AN INTERCESSION FOR THE HEROINE

Lucy, in an emotional scene, asks Richard to wait about their marriage, for his sake, for she is afraid of what his father will do to him upon having been defied. But Richard talks her out of her reservations, and by the end of the chapter, they have agreed that they will be married immediately, as Richard wishes.

> **Comment:** The action of this chapter is both moving and self-evident, and it is in Meredith's treatment, the predictable fruit of Sir Austin's unnatural System. Probably Richard is right, because he is, as he feels, surrounded by those who would prevent the marriage and separate him from Lucy. One should not draw from this part of the book the moral that a young man ought to be given a bit more freedom or he will punish his family by a secret marriage. This is much too simplistic a view.

CHAPTER XXXII: RELATES HOW PREPARATIONS FOR ACTION WERE CONDUCTED UNDER THE APRIL OF LOVERS

Ripton and Richard visit Lucy that morning, and Meredith takes the occasion for some **satire** of Ripton, who leads a more conventional and of course more worldly life in London than Richard would ever have done. But Meredith does not attribute Richard's superior behavior to the System; instead, it is in spite of the System that he has attained virtue.

Back at their rooms, Mrs. Berry, the landlady, moves more and more into the role Meredith has assigned her as Juliet's Nurse, as she looks after Lucy. There had been a slight difficulty when, in the park, where the three were riding that morning, Richard's uncle, Algernon, put in an unexpected and coincidental appearance. Richard thinks quickly and introduces Lucy to him as "Ripton's sister." Later, this kind of deception upsets Lucy, who is always honest and straightforward, for as Richard says, "she hates a lie." They take Mrs. Berry into their confidence regarding the plans for the elopement and everything else, except for telling their names.

Lucy has a long talk with Mrs. Berry, telling her of her apprehensions, and proving herself much more a child of simple nature than sophisticated art. Meanwhile, Ripton and Richard make arrangements for a clergyman and a marriage-license. Mrs. Berry gives them much help, for she has been experienced in helping others in such matters before. Richard sends Tom Bakewell back to Raynham for additional funds and his written request is honored. By the end of this chapter, all preparations for the marriage are set.

Comment: Richard never doubts for a moment that he must marry Lucy instantly, before she is taken away from him again for good. In this, Meredith presents his view that what he called in one of his great poems, *The Thrush in February*, "just instinct fed by valiant Blood," is operating here exactly as it should, and that the offense of attempting to suppress Nature is entirely Sir Austin's. Richard is behaving as he should, given the circumstances, and Sir Austin deserves nothing else.

CHAPTER XXXIII: IN WHICH THE LAST ACT OF A COMEDY TAKES THE PLACE OF THE FIRST

Here Richard is at the point of his irrevocable step of marriage to Lucy. Meredith uses the **metaphor** of Caesar's crossing the Rubicon: "Be your Rubicon big or small, clear or foul, it is the same: you shall not return." This implies the power of a man to make a freely-willed choice, and is thus in line with Meredith's philosophy of vitalism, discussed earlier. Richard is to cross "the River of his Ordeal." And Meredith approves of this. "Honest passion has an instinct that can be safer than conscious wisdom." This is what Meredith terms "Instinct speaking," and man can obey its dictates, and obey them freely.

Richard has arranged to meet his bride secretly at church at a quarter past eleven. Suddenly he encounters, during a stroll through the park, Mrs. Doria Forey and her daughter, Clare. He has not met them for a number of years, and now he is stuck, especially since Adrian is with them and is likely to become suspicious if he behaves in any way peculiarly. Richard spends what time he has telling Clare how much a certain other young man admires her. Then the hero, Richard, consults his watch and offers to leave, as he has a most pressing engagement. He has trouble breaking off. Mrs. Doria Forey tells Richard that she intends that Clare marry an older and more established man. Then Richard urgently says that he must go. When prevailed upon most importunately to stay, Richard suddenly says, "Good-bye," and leaves all of them standing there, amazed. This is after Mrs. Doria had jokingly wondered out loud what could be so important as to lead a young man to be so rude in taking his leave at eleven in the morning. A wedding? But he has dropped something, which Clare has picked up.

The "something" Richard has lost, which Mrs. Doria requires Clare to give her, is a wedding ring. It fits Clare, and Mrs. Doria draws the inference. Meanwhile, at the altar in the church, Richard and Lucy stand, with Ripton and Mrs. Berry for witnesses. Richard has lost his ring. But with quick resourcefulness, a second is provided and the marriage is concluded.

Comment: Meredith strikes precisely the right degree in terms of his tone in this chapter, between humor and seriousness. The marriage is the most important social culmination and social act there can be for Meredith, involving as it does the very quality of the future. With it, there is a change in the quality of the novel, and from this point it will become not joyous, but somber, for reasons which will manifest themselves quickly.

CHAPTER XXXIV: CELEBRATES THE BREAKFAST

This chapter refers to the wedding-breakfast. Lucy takes it as a poor and threatening omen that she has had to be married in another woman's wedding ring. It was Mrs. Berry's ring, and Lucy cannot return it to her; she will buy her another. As they are packing to go on their honeymoon journey to the Isle of Wight, Mrs. Berry asks for the ring, saying that it may be unlucky for Lucy. But Lucy cannot give it up, because Richard had said: "With this ring I thee wed." Ripton, meanwhile, has said that he will go down to tell Sir Austin of the wedding, but Richard cautions him positively not to do so until the next day, on the six o'clock train, and to give his father a letter he, Richard, has written him. Ripton is then to go to speak with Farmer Blaize, Lucy's uncle.

Mrs. Berry's touching and final gift to Lucy, as bride and groom ride away, is an old book, Dr. Kitchener on Domestic Cookery. Ripton, even, is properly impressed with all of the proceedings, and becomes somewhat inebriated on claret, telling Richard that he himself will probably not marry, as girls do not take to him.

Comment: This is one of the chapters that speaks for itself; artistically, it is beyond praise except that one may say that Meredith handles its unusual circumstances quite well in terms of its restraint and lack of sentimentality. Richard is decisive, as he should be, and is convinced that he is doing the right thing, even though he is defying his father's wishes. But the episode of the wedding ring, while humorous, is used as a foreteller of darker things to come.

CHAPTER XXXV: THE PHILOSOPHER APPEARS IN PERSON

Much of the wedding-cake is left and there is nobody to send it to. Ripton, in his intoxicated condition, tells Mrs. Berry who Richard is; his father's name is one of the oldest Baronetcies of England. Shortly thereafter, Adrian Harley appears at Mrs. Berry's house, having tracked down Richard. Adrian sees the wedding cake. The long arm of coincidence turns out to be just too long here, for when Adrian confirms that Richard is a Feverel of Raynham Abbey, Mrs. Berry admits that she had been at the Abbey herself. "I knew you when you was a boy that big, and wore jackets..." she says to Adrian. Adrian deduces that someone there was married very recently. Was it Ripton? At this point, the latter is sleeping off the effects of the wine. He concludes that it was Richard. Where has he gone? "To the Isle o'..." begins Mrs. Berry. Then common sense rescues her, and she says that she does not know. But she has already told Adrian enough.

Mrs. Berry is receiving a small pension from Sir Austin, and still will not permit herself to be swayed to tell more to Adrian. But he does not need to hear more, for the Isle of Wight is a favorite honeymoon spot. "So dies the System," thinks Adrian. At least, "he dies respectably in a marriage-bed, which is more than I should have foretold...." Adrian, thus, has been hypocritically serving his Chief, Sir Austin, without much credence in the System, as we have suspected all along.

Comment: This chapter straightforwardly advances the action quickly. The coincidence - that Mrs. Berry is the same girl whom Sir Austin had wept in front of, revealing his agony to a servant at that time; back in Chapter II, after his wife had left him - this is far-fetched, but, nevertheless it is in keeping with the somewhat jocular tone of the chapter.

CHAPTER XXXVI: PROCESSION OF THE CAKE

Adrian appears with some of the wedding cake, and gives it to Hippias Feverel. After beating about the bush, he tells Hippias that the cake was Richard's and that Richard was married that morning and is gone to spend his honeymoon on the Isle of Wight.

Adrian next encounters Captain Algernon Feverel, telling him the same thing and also giving him some cake. Algernon thinks that the bride was Thompson, the solicitor's daughter, but Adrian sets him right: it is Miss Desborough, "a Roman Catholic dairymaid." Finally, Adrian meets Mrs. Doria Forey, and tells her the - to her - disastrous, news. Is the marriage valid? Both Mrs. Doria and Brandon Forey, a barrister, are asked this by Adrian. Brandon says yes. Mrs. Doria is much more concerned with knowing where Richard is, so that perhaps Richard and Lucy can be separated and the marriage annulled. Mrs. Doria's view is that Richard must have been entrapped into the marriage by a designing woman, that he is under the legal age, and also, that her brother, Sir Austin, will never forgive him. The lawyer, Brandon, lists various ways to invalidate a marriage - if the man was under eighteen. Just then Clare interposes: "Richard is nineteen years and six months old today, Mama." Finally, seeing no other possibility, Mrs. Doria demands to be taken to see Mrs. Bessy Berry, from whose house Richard was married. She is brutal to Mrs. Berry, but Mrs. Doria treats her so because of the sudden shattering of all her schemes and plans to marry her daughter to Sir Austin's son and heir.

Comment: The suspense is somewhat heightened. Richard, as the result of Mrs. Berry's and Ripton's loose tongues, has already been located. If it were possible to locate him, frankly, before the consummation of his marriage, it would be legally possible, in nineteenth-century England, for the marriage to be annulled. Mrs. Doria knows this, and suggests that Richard be pursued and taken, by force if necessary. But as it will happen, this is not to eventuate.

CHAPTER XXXVII: NURSING THE DEVIL

Ripton Thompson has gone down to Raynham and delivered Richard's letter to Sir Austin, who says philosophically, "You see, Emmeline, it is useless to base any System on a human being." Mrs. Blandish is sympathetic, and takes Richard's part at the same time. Here Meredith injects some authorial comment: Sir Austin should have said, "never experimentalize with a human being...." For "he had experimented on humanity in the person of the son he loved as his life." Now he is attributing all of humanity's failings on his son. At once, a "Manichaean tendency," latent for years in Sir Austin, comes to the surface, and he nurses the Devil. This oblique reference is another of Meredith's Zoroastrian images; he means that Sir Austin is under the dominion of the dark spirit, Ahriman, in terms of his reaction to the marriage. The baronet speculates that Ripton, with his Wild Oats and his Miss Random, is morally sounder than Richard, because at least he did not plot to deceive his father.

Mrs. Blandish comes to Sir Austin as he sits through the night solitary, and asks that he forgive Richard. But he sees Richard, in marrying beneath him, as having repeated his cousin, Austin Wentworth's, "sin." She says that the situation is different; that Lucy is not the same kind of woman as Austin Wentworth's estranged wife, who was very ordinary.

The morning light dawns, and who should come with it but the butler, Heavy Benson. Sir Austin has not slept that night. The baronet asks for breakfast. He adds that Benson, the one believer at Raynham now in "the great Shaddock dogma," will not be returning there; he is to be discharged from service, but Sir Austin intends to make a provision for him. Benson is stunned.

Comment: Sir Austin does not really take the news well. In fact, his pride is hurt, as it had been when his wife left him - but instead of attributing her leaving him to his coldness, Sir Austin attributes both these actions to human corruption, and will not heed the sound advice of Mrs. Blandish.

CHAPTER XXXVIII: CONQUEST OF AN EPICURE

Richard and Lucy had been spending a month on the Isle of Wight, and there they had met a Mr. Morton, a gentleman who had been Sir Austin's friend, and was the uncle of Ralph, who was in love with Clare Forey; he was also the friend of Austin Wentworth. He introduces Richard to a Lady Judith Felle, who in turn introduces him to Lord Mountfalcon, a fashionable and time-wasting nobleman. Now Richard, coming out from under the influence of the System, is launched socially in "deep waters," as the Isle of Wight seems at the time to be the center, that July, of a very fashionable yachtsmen's set. Sir Austin, meanwhile, had at least come around to the extent that he is not withholding money from Richard; nor had he tried to contest the validity of the marriage. But he has shut his heart to Richard.

Adrian Harley appears at this point. He tells Richard how his father had taken the news of the marriage. Sir Austin had said little. Meanwhile, Mrs. Doria Forey, being foiled in a plan for Clare to marry a certain young man - Adrian does not elaborate - decides that she will marry an older one, and has chosen the man. Richard is horrified at such a loveless arrangement, and says that he will interfere with it. "Don't," is the one word of advice Adrian gives him. Adrian then talks to Lucy privately, while Richard is involved in a yacht race, and cautions her that perhaps it would be better if initially Richard should see his father alone. The arguments Adrian uses are quite convincing, for he can be convincing.

Richard is later quite against this idea, but Adrian has done his work well. He has already supplied the first object of discord, or at least difference of opinion, between husband and wife. Richard refuses to go to his father without Lucy. Lucy does not want to go, as a result of what Adrian has told her. Meanwhile, Sir Austin thinks that he, Richard, his own son, has refused to see him, and his heart is hardened still further.

It is Adrian who has the responsibility for this misunderstanding, and as empty of human consideration as he is, he would not have intended such harm to Richard, but by an ironic twist, he has done just what he should not with his argument to Lucy that she not accompany her husband. Finally, Lady Blandish, also with the best intentions in the world, writes to Richard: "Come instantly, and come alone." And Richard does this, against his better judgment.

> **Comment: Richard commits the innocent-enough mistake, surrounded as he is by well-wishers and people whom he trusts, such as Lady Blandish, of not trusting his instinct. He should not have come without Lucy, but he agreed to do so, and this will set in motion the final shocking catastrophe. Meredith implies that Richard's choice is free, but he knows less of the world than he should, due to his upbringing under the wretched System.**

CHAPTER XXXIX: CLARE'S MARRIAGE

Meanwhile, in town, three weeks after Richard's arrival without Lucy, Clare Forey is married to a Mr. John Todhunter, who is a gentleman of property and of whom Meredith says that it would have been more in order for him to marry the mother than the daughter. Clare has no choice in the matter. Mrs. Forey has seen that Clare had indeed fallen in love with Richard and was pining away, so finding it impossible to break up Richard's marriage with Lucy, she arranges a marriage for Clare as a kind of distraction. Also, she denounces Sir Austin and his System to his face. Sir Austin quietly tells his sister that it would be better to keep apart from him, which she assures him that she will do. Mrs. Doria does the wooing, and, shortly, the marriage is arranged.

Richard tries to talk her out of it, but Mrs. Doria is firm. "Let us see which turns out the best; a marriage of passion, or a marriage of common sense." Ralph Morton, who had been in love with Clare, is consulted by Richard, but Ralph tells him that it is Richard himself whom Clare has been in love with all along, and that as she does not care for him (Morton), he will not do such a thing as elope with her to prevent the marriage to Mr. Todhunter. Finally, Richard pleads with Clare not to go through with a loveless marriage. It is no use; she will do exactly as her mother wishes.

The effect of the preparations for Clare's marriage is pernicious, so far as Richard is concerned, for its distracts his mind. His father has not been ready to receive him, and after three weeks he still has not had his interview. Sir Austin's instructions to Adrian had been to "Take him about with you into every form of society." And Adrian, having his own concerns, had left Richard to the care of Mrs. Doria, his aunt. She attempted to divide Richard from his young wife.

Richard attends Clare's wedding, much against his will, but he refuses to be happy over the event. The marriage is a cold one from the beginning. Richard, after doing his best to prevent it, decides that he will leave London and return to his wife. Adrian is at his wit's end to detain him, when he meets the Honorable Peter Brayder, a side-kick or parasite of Lord Mountfalcon. He arranges for Brayder to have dinner with Richard and himself. Adrian says that he is not able to take Richard through the demimonde, though his father had wanted him to see all of society. Brayder, who is, as Meredith portrays him, no better than a panderer, has access to the sub-world of high society, and can take care of this for Adrian.

Adrian, finally, talks Richard into staying, by underhandedly appealing to his love for Lucy. If he, Richard, wants Sir Austin to receive his daughter-in-law, Lucy, he must do exactly as Adrian says, as Sir Austin is a "touchy" man who requires some deft management.

Comment: Richard consents, again contrary to his instinct, to stay in town with Adrian. The appeal Adrian has made to him is the only one which would have been successful, and Adrian was shrewd enough to know this. At this point, the action of the book is rapidly deepening, from tragicomedy toward pure tragedy. The innocent will suffer, and it should be noted how Meredith allows us to see that on the part of the principal tragic actors there is a great measure of free will; they are not mechanistically determined, though the tragedy will be none-the-less painful, in fact it will seem incredibly hard, if not viewed in the light of Meredith's poetic philosophy. "O life, how naked and how hard when known!" Meredith had written in A Ballad of Past Meridian. For what is to come here is as hard to accept as anything in nineteenth-century literature.

CHAPTER XL: A DINNER PARTY AT RICHMOND

Mrs. Bella Mount is seen driving a pair of gray horses in the park by Richard, in company with Adrian or The Honorable Peter Brayder (Meredith pointedly keeps repeating Brayder's courtesy title: he is the younger son of a peer, and therefore is entitled to be called "The Honorable," although, as his character is developed, we see that he is totally dishonorable.)

A plot has been arranged to introduce Richard to Mrs. Mount, the young lady who drives the horses in the park. Meanwhile, it is five weeks since Richard has come to town to see his father, and he writes him many times hoping that Sir Austin will see him. At this point, there is the demon of unconscious motivation on Sir Austin's part. He tells himself that he is "testing" Richard by keeping him in town and away from his wife. Actually, the testing is of a potentially very ugly kind, which Sir Austin will not admit to himself. Brayder proposes, on a morning in October, that Richard join him with Adrian at a dinner-party in Richmond. Ripton will accompany them; Richard reluctantly says yes.

The dinner is at Mrs. Mount's. Ripton drinks, rather as usual, and overhears Brayder and Bella Mount speaking. Mrs. Mount, who lives apart from her husband, is to have a large sum of money, on condition that she seduce "this young man." This young man in question turns out to be Richard, but Ripton does not gather this, for he is not quick enough. Ripton, nevertheless, realizes dimly that Richard oughtn't "to go near these people."

Comment: Richard's innocence and inexperience, in part the unhappy result of the System, is telling

against him at this point. The demi-monde, the "fast" society of London, of which Mrs. Mount and Brayder are a part, is a corrupt world which Richard should not enter, for he is too inexperienced. But he is being drawn to it.

THE ORDEAL OF RICHARD FEVEREL

TEXTUAL ANALYSIS

CHAPTERS 41-49

CHAPTER XLI: MRS. BERRY ON MATRIMONY

Richard, as the Hero, is now embarked "in the redemption of an erring beautiful woman." Were he more knowing, he would have realized that this was impossible under the circumstances; absolutely impossible. But his Systemic education had blinded him to certain social realities.

Meanwhile, Richard has a mind to return to his wife, as he should, but another legitimate problem interposes itself. Mrs. Doria has told him the story of his mother. He desires to hunt her out and take her back from her lover, the weak Somers. Lucy, when she learns of this, endorses the plan. Tom Bakewell is watching over Lucy. Ripton Thompson finds out Sandoe's place of residence.

Mrs. Berry sees Richard walking in the garden at Kensington arm-in-arm with a lady who is not his wife, and Mrs. Berry takes an instant dislike to the said lady, who is Mrs. Mount. "She has a boldface and is up to no good," thinks Mrs. Berry. Her instinct is right. When she learns that Richard has been away from his wife for nearly three months, she speaks to him as a mother. Richard finally promises that he will go down to see his wife by the end of the week. Meanwhile, he asks Mrs. Berry to receive a lady whom Richard will bring. This will be, it turns out, Richard's own mother; but Mrs. Berry does not know this now and suspects the worst.

> **Comment: Lady Feverel is finally brought, veiled, to Mrs. Berry's house. Richard has found her out and sternly removed her from the company of Diaper Sandoe, who is almost relieved to see her go. Meredith treats him as though he has little spirit, but one remembers the autobiographical implications of this passage.**

CHAPTER XLII: AN ENCHANTRESS

This is one of the most famous passages in the novel, in Meredith, and, indeed, in all of nineteenth-century English literature. It deals with the seduction of Richard by Mrs. Bella Mount, who is being paid shameful wages for this action, while convincing Richard that she is a fallen woman who requires to be saved.

A lurid glow, the **imagery** of the fires of a kind of Zoroastrian hell illuminate this passage. Of the Enchantress, Meredith's dry comment is "She never uttered an idea, or a reflection, but Richard thought her the cleverest woman he had ever met." Meredith's talent, at least outside his poetry proper, reaches perhaps its very highest level here. The chapter could stand as a play by itself; it proceeds so much by implication and is so developed in meaning by the interplay of the light-dark **imagery**, which

Meredith somehow associates with Zoroastrian dualism, that it can only be described as reaching a brilliance of the first rank.

Even Adrian, having seen that his scheme seems to be going too far, tries to talk Richard out of being seen any more with Mrs. Mount, but this only makes Richard more determined, because he thinks that the poor girl is being persecuted.

Bella is "the serpent of old Nile," and she knows how to play on Richard's sympathies. In the final fantastic scene, "a lurid splendor glanced about her like lights from the pit." In short, she seduces Richard; the scene is psychologically believable, at once appealing and painful in the extreme, and must be read closely to be appreciated.

> **Comment: Richard's fall was not exactly pre-ordained, in Meredith's view, but his wretched upbringing under the System had not prepared him to resist the Bella Mounts of this world.**
>
> **This is the longest chapter in the book, and as stated, artistically the most excellent. Was ever Hero in this fashion won? asks Meredith, paraphrasing the language of Shakespeare's *Richard III*. No - the scene is absolutely unique, and uniquely true, in English fiction of the century, inhibited as it was. This episode is too long to be analyzed in any detail. Though it deals with a seduction, the word is never mentioned, nor does Meredith have any prurient interest in the subject; in fact, in its psychological realism, it is modern in the extreme, nor could any but a Victorian reactionary have described it as other than highly moral in its meaning.**

CHAPTER XLIII: THE LITTLE BIRD AND THE FALCON: A BERRY TO THE RESCUE!

Lord Mountfalcon is still lingering on the Isle of Wight. He is in love with Richard's young wife, and we can deduce that it was Mountfalcon who had gotten Brayder to arrange the seduction of Richard, out of some notion that this might be the way for him to have Lucy. Lucy, very inexperienced, saw no harm in his visits. Brayder notifies his patron that Richard has fallen victim to Bella, who is evidently a cast-off mistress of Lord Mountfalcon.

Mountfalcon also tells Brayder that Lucy is pregnant. This is something that even her husband doesn't know. This may be dramatically not believable, but then, such subjects were treated with such reticence even between husband and wife in Victorian times that it is at least possible to believe that Lucy hadn't told Richard. Of course, there is another tragic **irony** here, for if Richard had known, he would have instantly come back to Lucy.

At this crucial point, not that Lucy is in danger of seduction by Mountfalcon, Mrs. Berry appears. She is appalled to hear that Richard is not there, for he has not been seen in London for fifteen days. Of course not! Having fallen victim to Mrs. Mount, he is with her, on the Sussex Coast, from whence she had written to Mountfalcon the cryptic message, beginning "My beautiful Devil!"

Mrs. Berry is here in the character of Juliet's Nurse, in *Romeo and Juliet*. Mrs. Berry takes charge, especially now that she realizes the situation that Lucy is in as the mother of Richard's child, with Richard not knowing. But that night, Mrs. Berry, who is determined to stay with Lucy and protect her, hears a noise outside in the garden. This noise leads in the day to her discovery of a footmark. Taking one of Richard's boots, she finds that the sole exactly fits the mark.

> **Comment: Even with Meredith's conformity to Victorian reticences, we can see that he is being quite frank here. He is writing of adult situations, for adults, and it is absolutely fantastic that he should then have been accused, then or now, of impropriety. He is simply honest, without sensationalism.**

CHAPTER XLIV: CLARE'S DIARY

A month elapsed, and Richard finally appears to his father. He tells him that he has taken the liberty to find his mother, and put her under his care. Mrs. Berry and Sir Austin finally arrange the long-postponed meeting of Richard with his wife, and he is death-pale when he sees her. Meanwhile, Clare is seriously ill, and Mrs. Doria must go to her; it is decided that Richard should accompany her.

Richard's countenance, as he speaks with his father, indicates a curious mixture of emotions. But part of the emotion is guilt. Meanwhile, Richard has arrived at Clare's home, to find her dead, of a malady which is not known, but which probably was a broken heart. On her finger are two wedding rings. One of these Richard recognizes; then he understands. It is the ring which he had bought for his own wedding to Lucy.

Richard now tastes unhappiness to the full, as he reads Clare's Diary, full of references to him. The tension is unbearable as Richard reads the diary and learns Clare's secret: that she had loved him only.

Comment: At this point, Richard feels unworthy to return to his wife, and tells Clare's mother that he is to go "seek for that which shall cleanse me." This sounds a bit like the Tannhauser legend, with which Meredith, through his German education, was probably familiar. But Richard's reference is to his feeling that he has betrayed his own wife. He must somehow make reparation. In medieval times, he would, like Tannhauser after his sojourn in the court of Venusberg and away from Elisabeth, go on a pilgrimage to obtain forgiveness. But now, Richard feels that no forgiveness can be his.

CHAPTER XLV: AUSTIN RETURNS

Austin Wentworth is now returned, after a five-year absence from Raynham and vicinity. Adrian briefs him on all that has happened, especially to Richard, and by now Richard's child has been born. It is a boy. All are, of course, pleased, because Raynham will have an heir. Richard has still not come to Raynham with his wife, nor has Sir Austin received them.

Austin comes to see Lucy at Mrs. Berry's residence. Lady Feverel is also in the house. But Richard is not. Come to Raynham with me - this is the message which Austin Wentworth, the saintly and oppressed man, brings to Lucy. She is to bring the child with her. It is Austin's thought to take the citadel of Raynham by storm, because he knows of the pride of the Feverels, father and son, and that nobody will ever yield first, unless there is a third party as intermediary.

The interview between Lucy and Sir Austin is satisfactory. Sir Austin capitulates before the vision of his grandson, and installs him in the very room which Richard had occupied as a boy. But Richard, still cursed by his feelings of guilt, is not yet back at Raynham. Meanwhile, Lady Feverel, Richard's mother, is also received at Raynham and the baronet grants her his pardon. Even Mrs. Berry sees her husband, who had left her so long ago, and this provides some Shakespearean-style comic relief, although Mrs. Berry has a natural dignity that makes her more a character of tragicomedy than of comedy.

Comment: The ghastly and far-reaching series of misunderstandings between all concerned at Raynham seems to be over. But the evil which has been done may linger on to blight at least some of the lives.

CHAPTER XLVI: NATURE SPEAKS

This, too, along with the chapter, "An Enchantress," is one of the most famous and most poetic portions of the novel. Richard, like Orestes in the great Greek tragic trilogy of Aeschylus, is figuratively pursued by the Furies - the Furies of his own feelings of guilt over his betrayal of his wife with Bella Mount. He does not know that he has been the victim of Lord Mountfalcon's plot.

This irrational reaction on the part of Richard is, Meredith implies, due to the effects of his father's System. It is at this point that the obstruction to further reconciliation is taking place within Richard. Richard is now with Lady Judith in the Rhineland, which of course Meredith knew well from his own sojourn there. And there, Austin Wentworth, as an emissary once again from Raynham, finds Richard.

Richard tells him that he cannot leave Lady Judith, and that she does not wish to part with him, "for his sake." "Why can't you go to your wife, Richard?" The answer the young man gives Austin is: "For a reason you would be the first to approve, Austin." That reason is Richard's guilt at the betrayal of his marriage vows.

They are on a bridge at Limburg on the Lahn, and Austin mentions to Richard that he is the father of a fine son. Richard hardly believes him, at first, and his lack of knowledge of this development is accounted for by the fact that Richard had burnt, unread, all letters from his father, from Lucy, and from Adrian, feeling that he is too disgraced and too contaminated even to reply. Further, both mother and child are at Raynham.

At this point Richard, in the beautiful and wild German forest, meditates on the situation within Nature. He experiences, in harmony with Nature, something which might be described as an enlightenment, and this is at the non-rational, even mystic level. At this, he has determined to return to Raynham, as though he has been cleansed by this moment of oneness with Nature.

Comment: This scene illustrates the Meridithian doctrine that when reason ("brain") fails man, the blood, or instinct, under the discipline of Nature, will come to assist him. Richard is saved by Nature, which the System would have perverted. It is described in poetic imagery perhaps second in the book only to that of Chapter XLII, "An Enchantress." The difficulty is that in that great chapter, there is what may be called the triumph of evil, of un-Nature, even in Zoroastrian terms. The question is whether it will be possible for the enlightenment which Richard has received here, in "Nature Speaks," to overcome the spells of the "Enchantress."

CHAPTER XLVII: AGAIN THE MAGIAN CONFLICT

The title and terminology of the chapter is once again Zoroastrian. The warfare between Good and Evil is to come to its **climax** shortly, and it is still not clear, in this long but extraordinarily fast-moving novel, which will win. With any other writer of his age, we might be able to have a fair idea of the outcome of the action, but not with Meredith. Any rate, at Raynham the news is heard abroad that the young Master, Richard, is returning finally.

Mrs. Berry tells, by indirection, the virtuous Lucy certain things about the duty of women to forgive their errant husbands - "the charity women should have towards sinful men." Meredith cannot go into any detail in this, given the **conventions** of his age, but what he says is to the point.

Now comes the climactic moment: the reunion of Richard with his family at Raynham. Again Richard is torn between two conflicting courses of action, outwardly trivial. He thinks of not going by his hotel for letters, but then he does - with that, the doom of someone very dear to him is sealed. Richard finds two letters. One is from Lucy, and its sentiments can be imagined. The second is from someone else - to be exact, Mrs. Bella Mount. Go home to your wife at once. This is her message, written with the best intentions possible. There is indeed bad news, for Bella Mount has found out about the Brayder-Mountfalcon plot to ruin Richard so that Lord Mountfalcon can take his wife from him. Bella Mount denies that she had taken any of their money, and advises Richard that the next time he sees Brayder, he should "cane him publicly." He instantly drives to Brayder's Club and demands the whereabouts of Lord Mountfalcon. Storming in to where the latter resides, Richard challenges him to a duel. Mountfalcon is really reluctant and is at a loss to know why this must be - he has already had new conquests and, as a matter of fact was actually innocent, although not in intention, toward Lucy. Ripton is asked by Mountfalcon to try to stop the duel. Now Ripton hurries down to Raynham. Richard is not coming that night, after all. They are all waiting up for him, but in vain.

Sir Austin has admitted that Lucy is altogether "a superior person" to be his son's wife. "I confess I should scarcely have hoped to find one like her." Sir Austin is even prepared to admit that his science, his System, cannot accomplish everything.

But then he comes - Richard is finally under his father's roof.

CHAPTER XLVIII: THE LAST SCENE

This is a close continuation of the one preceding, as action moves more and more rapidly toward the grand **catastrophe**, the tragic denouement. Richard has returned to Raynham. Lucy is very agitated, not only with the waiting but also with the uncertainty. "God...had spoken to him in the tempest," Meredith says of Richard. But there is still one final, self-imposed duty Richard must perform; he must meet Lord Mountfalcon on the "field of honor," in a duel. "Will you kill us all?" says Mrs. Doria to Richard, for she had heard, or overheard, a bit of what Ripton had told Adrian concerning the duel.

Richard goes to his wife, at long last. His father formally compliments him on his choice of a wife. But Richard asks Sir Austin: "A husband who has been unfaithful to his wife may go to her there, Sir?" Sir Austin is appalled. He cannot understand Richard, and he certainly has at this point no knowledge that it was, in part, his own doing that caused Richard to be seduced by Mrs. Bella Mount.

Richard has ordered Tom Bakewell to saddle his horse, for he will be leaving again that night. His interview with Lucy is almost unbearable in its poignancy, especially when he sees his son for the first time.

He tells his wife everything, and she forgives him instantly. He will never be parted from her again. But "two natures warred in his bosom, or it may have been the Magian Conflict still going on." He tells Lucy that he must leave once more, for two or three days. "He had not reckoned on her terrible suffering." But Richard's sense of honor, in conformity with the barbarous notions of the code duello, tears him away from his home and his wife, to go to meet Lord Mountfalcon.

> **Comment: Here the action of the book ends; what follows is a postscript, in Chapter XLIX, a letter written by one of the sympathetic characters, Lady Blandish, to the other saintly one, Austin Wentworth. Richard, by being too much swayed by the world, lacking the basis of instinctive wisdom which the System was intended to foster in him and instead only destroyed, was wrecked because the System had gone against the wisdom of Nature. Richard, up until the very last minute, could have done other than he did, but was locked into a code of worldly values by his father's System and his judgment was defective in this important, indeed vital, matter.**

CHAPTER XLIX: LADY BLANDISH TO AUSTIN WENTWORTH

This letter is almost in the nature of the comment of the Chorus of a classical Greek drama concerning the tragic action which has just gone before. It chronicles something so frightful and unbearable that it cannot be portrayed on the stage. In the letter to a kindred spirit, written by Lady Blandish, much abused by the world, but nevertheless a saint - one who understands reality at a very deep level - the significance of the action becomes clear, that there has been a great individual tragedy, leaving Richard's life in ruins, Lucy dead, and only their son to face the future and to give significance to their sufferings.

Richard, we learn, had fought a duel in France with Lord Mountfalcon, and was lying wounded, though not seriously, at a hamlet on the coast. The family immediately goes to him from Raynham.

Richard is not injured vitally, and several of the best physicians attend him; so he appears to be getting better.

But the French physician notices that Lucy seems to be ill, and he diagnoses the illness as cerebral fever - "brain fever." Exactly what this is maybe open to question, but we may say that Meredith means to attribute the death of the entirely innocent Lucy to the aggravation caused by the long separation, the uncertainty, and then the final anguish of the duel and Richard's wound.

Lady Blandish says that Sir Austin is still so blind that he cannot see the trouble he has caused with his System. "Come at once," Lady Blandish concludes to Austin Wentworth. "You will not be in time to see her. She will lie at Raynham. If you could you would see an Angel. He sits by her side for hours. I can give you no description of her beauty."

Comment: Only if one accepts the Meredithian philosophy of cosmic vitalism, with the notion that

the individual's life has significance only in terms of race progress, can one interpret *The Ordeal of Richard Feverel* as affirmative, as other than a hard and bitter young man's tragedy.

The grim ending of the novel can only be experienced, hardly discussed, for it is too painful for words. Considered not in isolation, however, but against the background of the philosophy provided principally in Meredith's poetry, one can see the consistency of Meredith's doctrine. He has performed the great, indeed the magnificent, tour de force of transmuting his own personal suffering into a universal experience.

A word should be said about the outcome of his consistently-maintained Zoroastrian or Magian metaphor. It may be that Meredith meant to imply, half-seriously, that at this point the world is under the dominance not of Ormuzd, but of the evil principle, Ahriman. Richard's life seems to be so; it is filled with a number of coincidences, all of which conduce to his being just a bit too early or too late or too eager or too reluctant, but in any case missing out on a lifetime of happiness. Just as Sir Austin has thought to live only for his son, and has totally botched the job with his System, so Richard will have to live for his son, and one can only hope and expect that Richard will be better at his all-important task of providing for the future of the race. We guess that he will be better, at the same time as we wonder whether there is any future for Richard, the disaster seeming to be so total.

Austin Wentworth, who hears all, is the kind of unobtrusive but healing personality in whom all confide, and it falls to his lot to see the end, or to hear of it from Lady Blandish, who has utterly lost faith in Sir Austin as a wise man. She is no longer interested in Sir Austin, and she recognizes in Austin Wentworth the model of behavior which she had thought to see in the baronet. But Sir Austin is punished enough, in this great and tragic event with which the novel ends, in a triumph of evil only redeemed by the existence of the next generation, in the form of Richard and Lucy's son, who may surpass the generation of his parents. This is only as affirmative as Meredith can be, but in the terms of the Meredithian philosophy, it must content us.

THE ORDEAL OF RICHARD FEVEREL

CHARACTER ANALYSES

RICHARD FEVEREL

The titular hero, he is an open and honest young man, physically very attractive, a son of the English aristocracy. He has a good mind, and he seems indeed to live up to the English aristocratic ideal, modeled on that of classical civilization, of a sound mind in a sound body. However, Richard has fallen afoul of his father's repressive System of education, and, in battling its effects, he loses what means more to him than his own life. Even his name, Feverel, suggests passion and fever. He is Romeo to his Lucy's Juliet, and the basic story is a Shakespearean one, deepening from tragicomedy to tragedy. Richard's "Ordeal," formally Woman, is actually his father's warped and warping System.

LUCY DESBOROUGH FEVEREL

The niece of Farmer Blaize, whose rick Richard and Ripton burn down. She is the daughter of a Royal Navy Lieutenant, and is much above her uncle socially. One can visualize her great and artless beauty (in contrast to the tainted and artful beauty of the

"Enchantress," her unknown rival, Mrs. Bella Mount). Lucy is of a Roman Catholic family and descent, unusual in this stratum of English society, especially of the landed country families of the period, but Meredith seems to have introduced the fact of Lucy's Catholicism simply to provide additional motivation for Richard's father's objections to her as his son's prospective wife. Lucy becomes the entirely innocent victim of Sir Austin Feverel's System, when she dies of "brain-fever" leaving Richard with their infant son.

SIR AUSTIN FEVEREL

The proprietor of Raynham Abbey and estate, a considerable figure in the society of his county, and with a very large income, all of which Richard is to inherit. As the eldest son, under the English law of primogeniture, he has become the head of the family. Having lost his wife through her running away with the failed poet and artist, Denzil Somers (Diaper Sandoe), Sir Austin withdraws into himself and becomes a kind of wit and philosopher, condensing many of his maxims and aphorisms into a book, originally published anonymously, called *The Pilgrim's Scrip*. The essence of his offense or crime against Richard is his treating his son as an object, rather than as an inviolate and sovereign personality. Sir Austin is the most fully characterized figure in the novel; the complexity of his character exceeds that of his son. In many ways, the book is his tragedy rather than Richard's, and in this sense it is well to recall the title. For Richard's "Ordeal" is his father and the System, which does not give him the equipment he needs to act prudently. Several of Sir Austin's actions are much misguided, to say the least, as when he advises Adrian to take Richard through town to see the London dens of vice.

LADY FEVEREL

Sir Austin's estranged wife. She is a shadowy figure, presented as suffering greatly; she had run away with Denzil Somers. Richard brings her back to Raynham. It is unlikely that she is actually reconciled with her husband, though she is forgiven by him. Historically, her character is based by Meredith on his own first wife, Mary Ellen Peacock.

DENZIL SOMERS ("DIAPER SANDOE")

Sir Austin's best friend, a distinctly third-rate poet and painter who had accepted Sir Austin's hospitality at Raynham and then run off with Lady Feverel, giving rise to Sir Austin's contempt for women. He is presented as a very weak and ineffectual character, who offers no resistance when Richard comes to bring his mother home.

ALGERNON FEVEREL

Sir Austin's brother, an uncle of Richard; he is a rather humorless character, very much interested in sports. He is a former Army officer.

HIPPIAS FEVEREL

Another of Richard's uncles, a "heavy" and somewhat ponderous type who sometimes serves as a sounding board for his brother's aphorisms.

MRS. DORIA FOREY

Sir Austin's widowed sister, who lives at the Abbey with him; she is the mother of Clare, and has a deep design of marrying off her daughter to Richard, even though they are cousins. She is the female counterpart to Sir Austin, and in too closely managing Clare's life and forcing Clare to be married to a middle-aged man who she does not love, Mrs. Doria, as Meredith usually calls her, is ensuring the same kind of **catastrophe** as Sir Austin brings about with his treatment of Richard. She is sometimes called Mrs. Battledore, and Clare is called "the fair Shuttlockiana." This refers to the view of the Feverels that Mrs. Doria is playing a kind of Badminton game, with Clare as the shuttlecock, beaten back and forth by the racquets of social and economic ambition.

CLARE FOREY

The tragic daughter of Mrs. Doria. Richard's cousin. Very deeply in love with Richard, she is married by her mother to a rather dull gentleman, many years older than herself, Mr. John Todhunter. She dies, also impliedly of a broken heart, leaving a diary which tells everything about her secret and hopeless longing for Richard. She is a foil and counterpart to Richard, also the victim of a parent's scheming or false ideas.

EMMELINE, LADY BLANDISH

As her name implies, she is exerting her "blandishments" on Sir Austin; she is a guest at Raynham, and desires to marry Sir Austin. However, Lady Blandish is by no means a shallow character. She had thought that Sir Austin was a wise man who understood women, but by the end of the book she has realized his emptiness and self-deception, as she expresses in the magnificent final letter written to Austin Wentworth concerning the **catastrophe**. Lady Blandish is one of the two "sympathetic" supporting characters, the other being Austin Wentworth; she is quite sensible, as well as sensitive to the realities of human life, and is used by Meredith somewhat as a detached observer, as well as an effective character who can actually help others.

FARMER BLAIZE

An "honest English yeoman" farmer, the neighbor of Sir Austin Feverel and the uncle of Lucy Desborough. He is a type character, not a rounded three-dimensional one, who represents the English countryside; and he is the victim of Richard's and Ripton's rick-burning plot, after having whipped Richard for poaching on his land. Basically, he is an honest man.

TOM BAKEWELL

A farmhand of Blaize, who executes the rick-burning for Richard, is apprehended and nearly transported for this offense, but instead becomes Richard's trusted personal servant.

RIPTON THOMPSON

Richard's best friend, the son of the family lawyer, or solicitor, Mr. Thompson. He goes through a number of adventures with Richard, and helps to arrange the marriage with Lucy in strict secrecy. He is contrasted with Richard in that he is the result of a conventional and worldly upbringing. Meredith clearly makes the social distinction between the two young men for purposes of contrast; Richard is of the aristocracy, while Ripton is middle-middle class.

AUSTIN WENTWORTH

A nephew of Sir Austin, he is the son of one of Sir Austin's sisters and of a Colonel Wentworth. He is either ignored or despised or both by many in the novel because he had married unwisely and beneath him, and for love, and because the girl had turned out to be unworthy. Actually, he is nearly a saint; he possesses the kind of healing personality which leads people to like and trust him. It falls to his lot to rescue Richard from the consequences of his actions, based on the unwisdom of the System, but he cannot save Lucy, and it is to him that the final letter of Lady Blandish is addressed, chronicling the catastrophe.

HEAVY BENSON

The Feverel butler, a dour and humorless man who is, like his master Sir Austin, also a misogynist, as a result of his wife having deserted him. Finally discharged by Sir Austin.

ADRIAN HARLEY

Also called "the wise youth," a hedonist and discreet sensualist, who is always making wise jests but who is basically for himself and cannot really help Richard when he needs help. Adrian is the confidant, and does some of the dirty work, of Sir Austin;

he is also a nephew of Sir Austin, and lives at Raynham with the rest of the curious assemblage there.

MRS. BERRY

As a young girl, a family servant of the Feverels, she had been sent away by Sir Austin but given a small pension, as she had seen the baronet in a moment of agonized weakness, the result of his chagrin over his failed marriage. She plays "Juliet's Nurse" in this *Romeo-and-Juliet* story; she runs lodgings in London, to which Richard brings both Lucy and his mother. A very kindly soul, and a great comic character who has innate dignity, nevertheless.

THE BANTAM

Another farmhand of Farmer Blaize, who gives evidence against Tom Bakewell in the trial resulting from the latter's rick-burning.

MRS. BELLA MOUNT

A beautiful and corrupt girl of the London demi-monde, a glorified society prostitute, though she is never referred to directly as such. The "Enchantress" in the most famous chapter of the book, she seduces Richard at the behest of Lord Mountfalcon, whose mistress she had been at one time. But even she falls eventually under the spell of Richard's innate goodness and his soundness of character, and wishes that she had not hurt him - when it is rather too late to do anything about it.

LORD MOUNTFALCON

An aristocratic and corrupt playboy of London society, who decides to seduce Lucy. But just as Bella Mount is eventually charmed into respect by Richard's innocence and nobility, so Mountfalcon is charmed by Lucy, abandoning his design against her after it is too late. Reluctantly he fights a duel with Richard and wounds him, though not seriously. This indirectly brings about Lucy's death.

THE HONORABLE PETER BRAYDER

The younger son of an aristocratic family, hence his title, used ironically by Meredith. He is a hanger-on of Lord Mountfalcon, who is a go-between in the underworld of the peer's dark pleasures; he is actually a society panderer. His name suggests the "bray" of a jackal, which he is - a social jackal; he is a "running-dog" of a corrupt aristocracy.

RALPH MORTON

A young man who had been in love with Clare Forey, but who learns the truth about Clare's passion for Richard, of which she dies after her marriage to another. He joins the Army, and he proves himself as a good friend to Richard.

THE ORDEAL OF RICHARD FEVEREL

AN ESSAY ON THE RELATION OF MEREDITH'S POETRY TO HIS FICTION

....

We have mentioned earlier that Meredith is the most poetic of nineteenth-century English novelists, and elevated the poetic novel to a degree that has hardly ever been surpassed. His style, as well as the intellectual content of his works, is distinctive. His great contemporary, Thomas Hardy, was also a poet as well as a novelist and also wrote philosophical poetry as his reaction to a troubled age. But Meredith's poetry, difficult as much of it is to understand, at its best far surpasses even the most superior poetic efforts of Hardy. Hardy, after all, was trained as an architect, and had what might be described as an architectonic approach to the problems of the construction of the novel.

In the Bibliography there is a special section listing all of Meredith's poems and volumes of poetry, together with the principal critical works useful in dealing with the poetry. As can be seen from the list, Meredith published a good deal of poetry, and these volumes appeared at the same time as his works of fiction were being written. Whether Meredith was a poet of the very first rank is open to question on a number of grounds, but at his best, he reached great heights of poetic achievement. His sequence of fifty sixteen-line "quasi-sonnets" entitled *Modern Love* is among the most excellent and original poetry of the Victorian age, astonishingly modern, by twentieth-century standards, in its insights into human relationships and its fresh **imagery** and symbolic statement.

In the selection of his poetry below, one rather long poem, *The Thrush in February*, is presented with a detailed explication which has attempted to weave in the ideas of the poem with those expressed in Meredith's novels, especially in *The Ordeal of Richard Feverel*. For, while this poem was written many years after *The Ordeal*, its ideas are consistent with those developed in that novel, and help to comment upon and to explain the novel.

Because the language is unusual, fresh, and original, there must be explication in depth of *The Thrush in February*, which might be described as a poem proceeding from Nature to the Soul; from simple natural description to the elevation of a natural fact into a spiritual symbol. The poem is thus technically in the tradition of both philosophical Idealism, which takes natural facts as analogies for spiritual realities, and of philosophical Naturalism (or rather of theological Naturalism), which denies the miraculous and supernatural in religion - for in this poem there are explicit denials of the latter, making its position affirmative of Life without any externally-based religious sanctions. One thing the poem is not "about" is the thrush, any more than Keats's *Ode on a Grecian Urn* or *Ode to a Nightingale* are "about" an Urn or a nightingale. For if the latter two poems have involved in their meanings the equivalence of Truth and Beauty and the awful search of man for some permanence in the midst of an apparently ceaselessly changing universe that seems basically hostile to him, *The Thrush in February* has as its **theme** the acceptance and even joyful embracing by man of reality; of what is, in Meredith's view, the nature of reality, hard though it may seem.

The other poems included are the great poem XXX from *Modern Love*, the very well-known **sonnet** *Lucifer in Starlight*, with its concentrated thematic statement of the omnipresence of a natural law that is not necessarily a divine law (even though Meredith uses the theological figure of Lucifer as a point of focus - for in this poem Lucifer simply symbolizes the forces of darkness and disorder), and finally two poems, *A **Ballad** of Past Meridian* and *Woodland Peace*, both involving Death, Change, and man's appropriate reaction to them.

The language of these poems, especially of *The Thrush in February*, is elliptical and compressed. In the very first **stanza** of this poem, Meredith uses "valentine" as a verb, i.e., "to valentine," which says much, but is surely the only use in quite this compressed manner in all of English poetry of a word which is customarily a noun. The texts of these poems are given here for convenience in considering them together with the explications and commentaries presented below. It should be kept in mind that thematically, *The Thrush in February* and *The Ordeal of Richard Feverel* are very closely related.

THE THRUSH IN FEBRUARY [1885]

I know him, February's thrush,
And loud at eve he valentines
On sprays that paw the naked bush
4 Where soon will sprout the thorns and bines.

Now ere the foreign singer thrills
Our vale his plain-song pipe he pours,
A herald of the million bills;
And heed him not, the loss is yours.

My study, flanked with ivied fir
And budded beech with dry leaves curled'
Perched over yew and juniper,
He neighbours, piping to his world: -

The wooded pathways dank on brown,
The branches on grey cloud a web,
The long green roller of the down,
An image of the deluge-ebb: -

And farther, they may hear along
The stream beneath the poplar row.
By fits, like welling rocks, the song
20 Spouts of a blushful Spring in flow.

But most he loves to front the vale
When waves of warm South-western rains
Have left our heavens clear in pale,
With faintest beck of moist red veins:

Vermilion wings, by distance held
To pause aflight while fleeting swift:
And high aloft the pearl inshelled
Her lucid glow in glow will lift;

A little south of coloured sky;
Directing, gravely amorous,
The human of a tender eye
Though pure celestial on us:

Remote, not alien; still, not cold;
Unraying yet, more pearl than star;
She seems a while the vale to hold
In trance, and homelier makes the far.

Then Earth her sweet unscented breathes;
An orb of lustre quits the height;
And like broad iris-flags, in wreaths
40 The sky takes darkness, long ere quite.

His Island voice then shall you hear,
Nor ever after separate
From such a twilight of the year
Advancing to the vernal gate.

He sings me, out of Winter's throat,
The young time with the life ahead;
And my young time his leaping note
Recalls to spirit-mirth from dead.

Imbedded in a land of greed,
Of mammon-quakings dire as Earth's,
My care was but to soothe my need;
At peace among the little worths.

To light and song my yearning aimed;
To that deep breast of song and light
Which men have barrenest proclaimed;
As 'tis to senses pricked with fright.

So mine are these new fruitings rich
The simple to the common brings;
I keep the youth of souls who pitch
60 Their joy in this old heart of things:

Who feel the Coming young as aye,
Thrice hopeful on the ground we plough;
Alive for life, awake to die;
One voice to cheer the seedling Now.

Full lasting is the song, though he,
The singer passes: lasting too,
For souls not lent in usury,
The rapture of the forward view.

With that I bear my senses fraught
Till what I am fast shoreward drives.
They are the vessel of the Thought.
The vessel splits, the Thought survives.

Nought else are we when sailing brave,
Save husks to raise and bid it burn.
Glimpse of its livingness will wave
A light the senses can discern

Across the river of the death,
Their close. Meanwhile, O twilight bird
Of promise! bird of happy breath!
80 I hear, I would the City heard.

The City of the smoky fray;
A prodded ox, it drags and moans:
Its Morrow no man's child; its Day
A vulture's morsel beaked to bones.

It strives without a mark for strife;
It feasts beside a famished host:
The loose restraint of wanton life.
That threatened penance in the ghost.

Yet there our battle urges; there
Spring heroes many: issuing thence,
Names that should leave no vacant air
For fresh delight in confidence.

Life was to them the bag of grain,
And Death the weedy harrow's tooth.
Those warriors of the sighting brain
Give worn Humanity new youth.

Our song and star are they to lead
The tidal multitude and blind
From bestial to the higher breed
100 By fighting souls of love divined.

They scorned the ventral dream of peace
Unknown in nature. This they knew:
That life begets with fair increase
Beyond the flesh, if life be true.

Just reason based on valiant blood
The instinct bred afield would match
To pipe thereof a swelling flood,
Were men of Earth made wise in watch.

Though now the numbers count as drops
An urn might bear, they father Time.
She shapes anew her dusty crops;
Her quick in their own likeness climb.

Of their own force do they create;
They climb to light, in her their root.
Your brutish cry at muffled fate
She smites with pangs of worse than brute

She, judged of shrinking nerves, appears
A Mother whom no cry can melt;
But read her past desires and fears,
120 The letters on her breast are spelt.

A slayer, yea, as when she pressed
Her savage to the slaughter-heaps,
To sacrifice she prompts her best:
She reaps them as the sower reaps.

But read her thought to speed the race,
And stars rush forth of blackest night:
You chill not at a cold embrace
To come, nor dread a dubious might.

Her double visage, double voice,
In oneness rise to quench the doubt.
This breath, her gift, has only choice
Of service, breathe we in or out.

Since Pain and Pleasure on each hand
Led our wild steps from slimy rock
To yonder sweeps of gardenland,
We breathe but to be sword or block.

The sighting brain her good decree
Accepts; obeys those guides, in faith,
By reason hourly fed, that she,
140 To some the clod, to some the wraith,

Is more, no mask; a flame, a stream.
Flame, stream, are we, in mid career
From torrent source, delirious dream,
To heaven-reflecting currents clear.

And why the sons of Strength have been
Her cherished offspring ever; how
The Spirit served by her is seen
Through Law; perusing love will show.

Love born of knowledge, love that gains
Vitality as Earth it mates,
The meaning of the Pleasures, Pains,
The Life, the Death, illuminates.

For love we Earth, then serve we all;
Her mystic secret then is ours:
We fall, or view our treasures fall,
Unclouded, as beholds her flowers

Earth, from a night of frosty wreck,
Enrobed in morning's mounted fire,
When lowly, with a broken neck,
160 The crocus lays her cheek to mire.

Text: *The Poetical Works of George Meredith*, ed. with notes by G. M. Trevelyan (London: Constable & Co., 1919), pp. 327–31.]

A BALLAD OF PAST MERIDIAN [1876]

I

Last night returning from my twilight walk
I met the grey mist Death, whose eyeless brow
Was bent on me, and from his hand of chalk
He reached me flowers as from a withered bough:
O Death, what bitter nosegays givest thou!

II

Death said, I gather, and pursued his way.
Another stood by me, a shape in stone,
Sword-hacked and iron stained, with breasts of clay,
And metal veins that sometimes fiery shone:
O Life, how naked and how hard when known!

III

Life said, As thou hast carved me, such am I.
Then memory, like the nightjar on the pine,
And sightless hope, a woodlark in night sky,
Joined notes of Death and Life till night's decline:
Of Death, of Life, those inwound notes are mine.

[Text: Trevelyan, p. 205]

MODERN LOVE - XXX [1862]

What are we first? First, animals; and next
Intelligences at a leap; on whom
Pale lies the distant shadow of the tomb,
And all that draweth on the tomb for text.
Into which state comes Love, the crowning sun:
Beneath whose light the shadow loses form.
We are the lords of life, and life is warm.
Intelligence and instinct now are one.
But nature says: "My children most they seem
When they least know me: therefore I decree
That they shall suffer." Swift doth young Love flee,
And we stand wakened, shivering from our dream.
Then if we study Nature we are wise,
Thus do the few who live but with the day:
The scientific animals are they. -
Lady, this is my sonnet to your eyes.

LUCIFER IN STARLIGHT [1883]

On a starred night Prince Lucifer uprose.
Tired of his dark dominion swung the fiend
Above the rolling ball in cloud part screened,
Where sinners hugged their spectre of repose.
Poor prey to his hot fit of pride were those.
And now upon his western wing he leaned.
Now his huge bulk o'er Afric's sands careened,
Now the black planet shadowed Arctic snows.
Soaring through wider zones that pricked his scars
With memory of the old revolt from Awe,
He reached a middle height, and at the stars,
Which are the brain of heaven, he looked, and sank.
Around the ancient track marched, rank on rank,
The army of unalterable law.

WOODLAND PEACE [1870]

Sweet as Eden is the air,
And Eden-sweet the ray.
No Paradise is lost for them
Who foot by branching root and stem,
5 And lightly with the woodland share
The change of night and day.

Here all say,
We serve her, even as I:
We brood, we strive to sky,
10 We gaze upon decay,
We wot of life through death,
How each feeds each we spy;
And is a tangle round,
Are patient; what is dumb

15 We question not, nor ask
   The silent to give sound,
   The hidden to unmask,
   The distant to draw near.

   And this the woodland saith:
20 I know not hope or fear;
   I take whate'er may come;
   I raise my head to aspects fair.
   From foul I turn away.

   Sweet as Eden is the air,
25 And Eden-sweet the ray.

Critical Background: Alice Brandreth Butcher, in her *Memoirs of George Meredith*, recounts that Meredith once told her, apropos of a discussion of his literary reputation that "...he thought his poems would outlive his novels, even though during his own lifetime they were hardly read at all." Lady Butcher was no Boswell, and perhaps it was her very naivete which led Meredith occasionally to confide in her. "I think Mr. Meredith cares a great deal about his poems, as into them he has packed, condensed, and compressed all his philosophy of life," she wrote in the Memoirs.

Meredith's poetry has been largely ignored by critics, and the one book dealing specifically with the poetry is, significantly enough, by an historian; a great historian who, it appears, finds in the work of Meredith the fullest expression of what he conceives to be the English national genius, and is fascinated by him for this reason. George M. Trevelyan's book, published during the poet's lifetime, is outdated, for one reason because it says very little about the intellectual background of the poetry. Facts about Meredith's life and literary relationships are known today which were unavailable in 1906. But Trevelyan, in his "Introduction," stated a thesis which deserves serious consideration, when he wrote:

> When Mr. Meredith's work comes up for judgment by a distant posterity, novels and poems will be taken into account together. His poems are not the product of one side of his nature, and his novels of another. The more carefully we read them both, the dearer it becomes that the novels are the work of the poet, and the poems the work of the novelist. No other novels are so lyrical in spirit, no other poems so richly endowed with a novelist's insight into character and emotion. In both we get, though in different degrees, the same ethical and philosophical ideas, the same intricate psychology, the same appeal to the intellectual in us, the same wealth of imagination, the same perpetual torrent of metaphor, illuminated by flashes of the same exquisite beauty, varied by darts of the same critical but kindly humour, troubled by the same faults of uncouth and obscure expression.

Meredith is a novelist and a poet of ideas who, by virtue of his ideas and of his manner of expressing them, generally arouses in his readers one of three reactions: great enthusiasm, extreme dislike, or simple puzzlement and bewilderment. These latter two reactions are about equally directed toward the form and the content of the Meredithian poem or novel. Thus, Sir Max Beerbohm could write a **parody** of Meredith in the *Christmas Number* of the *Saturday Review* for 1896, entitled *The Victory of Aphasia Ghibberish*:

> In the heart of insular Cosmos, remote by some scores of leagues of hodge-trod arable or pastoral - not more

than half a snuff-pinch to gaping tourists' nostrils accustomed to inhalation of prairie winds, but enough for perspective - from these marginal sands, trident-scraped, we are to fancy, by a helmeted Dame Abstract, familiarly profiled on discs of current bronze, price of a loaf for humbler maws disdainful of Gallic side-dishes for the titillation of choicer palates, stands Ghibberish Park, a house of some pretentions, mentioned at Runnymede, with the spreading exception of wings given to it in latter times by Daedalean monsters not to be balked of billiards or traps for Terpsichore, and owned for unbroken generations by a healthy line of procreant Ghibberishes, to the undoing of collateral branches eager for the birth of a female.

While critical response to Meredith's style has often been hostile, the response to the substance of his work has tended to show puzzlement. Thus Paul Elmer More, writing on Meredith in *Shelburne Essays, Second Series* (1905), said:

Richard Feverel holds the mind from first to last on a single problem (and that, by the way, a fairly disagreeable one), and every incident is made to bear on its development. There seems to be one aspect - the sexual relation - to human life; and this is presented without any of the alleviating circumstances of genuine tragedy.

Proceeding to an analysis of the later novels, Professor More said in part:

Clara Middleton and Diana, with their feverish attempt at revolt, and their final succumbing in marriage with a character of placid but undeveloped strength, are perhaps his most perfect creations. But I hasten to take leave of this perilous subject, and with it of Mr. Meredith.

More's essay may be taken as the type of those critical works which show little understanding of Meredith, and no sympathy with his purpose.

One final critical opinion may stand for the reaction of the reader who finds Meredith attractive, moving, but very puzzling. On 30 June, 1885, Barrett Wendell wrote to Lindsay Swift concerning *The Ordeal of Richard Feverel*:

> I don't know when I have been so stirred by a book - hatefully, horribly stirred. Hatefully, I say, because somehow I feel that the whole thing is too dreadful, that there is no real need of all the tragedy. There is cause and effect enough, logic enough, for anybody; yet there are just those unlucky accidents which an artist may cast aside. And without them there might have been in this great symphony a final harmony. Why must the last note be so harsh a discord?
> Yet, after all, my very protests show the power that this book has....

Discord: So far we have three representative criticisms of Meredith's work: first, an indictment of his style on the grounds that it is so involved, crabbed, and elliptical that it creates the impression of being mere nonsense, *The Victory of Aphasia Ghibberish*; second, a fear (less common today than in 1905) that Meredith is overly naturalistic in his treatment of fundamental human relationships; and, finally, a sincere puzzlement as to what Meredith is about, due to a lack of knowledge of Meredith's ethical philosophy and of the intellectual and scientific backgrounds of this philosophy. "Why must the last note be so harsh a discord?" This is a question which has been asked not only by readers of *The Ordeal of Richard Feverel*. For there are disquieting "notes of discord" in many of the novels: Diana's marriage to Warwick, the death of Sigismund Alvan in *The Tragic Comedians*; the career of Nevil Beauchamp, the great mistake which Lord Fleetwood made in *The Amazing Marriage*; the pig-headedness of Lord Ormont in his treatment of his wife in Lord Ormont and his Aminta. This question may be answered only by reference to Meredith's poetry - that to understand the Meredithian novel, we must have some knowledge of what Meredith's poetry is, in terms of its intellectual content, its form, its range of themes. Meredith must be taken literally when he said that he thought his poetry would outlive his fiction. The notion of approaching Meredith's novels by way of poetry is not a particularly new one, as may be seen from Professor Trevelyan's book. But this book falls down in its examination of the background of the poetry; it fails to set Meredith within a tradition, although it is still valuable for its enthusiastic approach and its analysis of individual poems. And it devotes relatively little space to the Meredith novels. Lionel Stevenson's chapter on *Meredith in Darwin among the Poets* (1932) is a very useful background study of the poetry, and the same may be said of the section dealing with Meredith in Joseph Warren Beach's book, *The Concept of Nature in Nineteenth-Century Poetry* (1936). But neither of these books relates the poetry to the novels in any detail. Indeed, there is one article which takes the specific approach that Meredith's poetry can cast light on the novels. This article, "The Meaning of Egoism in George Meredith's *The Egoist*," by Richard B. Hudson, appeared in *Nineteenth-Century Fiction*, December, 1948. The burden of this article is that if we read *The Egoist* without "an understanding of what egoism stood for in Meredith's philosophy," we find it nothing but a boring task. Hudson begins by saying:

George Meredith's *The Egoist*, published in 1879, is a novel of life among the landed gentry in which a wealthy member of that class is forced to undergo humiliation because of his preposterous absorption in himself, his concern for his own comfort and convenience, and his appearance to the world at large. His nemesis is not an aroused and militant proletariat, not an indignant society, but the Comic Spirit and her attendant imps, who catch him off guard and apply the corrective of laughter. The casual reader might infer that there is no more to the novel.

The article then goes on to discuss what Meredith meant by the word "egoism," which, as Hudson shows, is a key concept in the Meredithian ethical system, and he makes his case with reference to such poems as *The Woods of Westermain*, *Hard Weather*, and *The Test of Manhood*. It is this technique, or method: the application of Meredith's poetry to the study of his novels, which can be most fruitful in considering Meredith's greatest novel.

We have been talking about Meredith's ethical system as expressed in his poetry. Yet one must not give the impression that Meredith was simply a **didactic** versifier. His poetry is definitely a poetry of ideas, and it is difficult to read. At times, the **syntax** and choice of words sound like *The Victory of Aphasia Ghibberish*. And in the considerable body of Meredith's poems, it is easy to find some things which are mediocre or worse.

T. S. Eliot, in his essay on the **Metaphysical** *Poets* (1921), said:

The possible interests of a poet are unlimited; the more intelligent he is the better; the more intelligent he is the more likely that he will have interests: our only condition is that he turn them into poetry, and not merely meditate on them poetically.

At his best, there is an extraordinary balancing of thought and emotion in Meredith's philosophic poetry: "a direct sensuous apprehension of thought, or a re-creation of thought into feeling," to use the well-known phrase with which Mr. Eliot described the technique of Donne.

Meredith has an ideal, based on the ethical system which he developed for himself under the impact of nineteenth-century evolutionary theory. In a sense, both his poetry and his novels are highly **didactic**, but in an indirect manner for, as he wrote in *The Ordeal of Richard Feverel*: "The born preacher we feel instinctively to be our foe. He may do some good to the wretches that have been struck down, and lie gasping; he rouses deadly enmity in the strong."

While the Meredithian novel will define an ideal by indirection or dramatically, through the illustration of character in action, the poetry works more directly through statement based on the authority of the Carlylean poet-prophet. The best way to illustrate what is meant is to examine a representative longer poem of Meredith. We have here selected *The Thrush in February* not because it is Meredith's greatest poem. It is not, by any means. But it is thoroughly characteristic of Meredith in terms of its form and **syntax**, and in its intellectual content. We will make use, in this explication of the poem, of what Brooks and Warren called "message-hunting" in a pejorative sense in *Understanding Poetry*, but how else can one deal with the poetry of ideas? To discuss a poem of this nature without considering the ideas it expresses would be worthless.

Meredith's ethical system can be approached in terms of the characteristic vices it holds up to the ridicule of the Comic Spirit for a very serious end. These vices are not necessarily those which the Christian religion attacks, but then Meredith, as we know, rejected orthodox religion early, at the Moravian school at Nieuwied. His feeling about life was essentially a religious one, but the highly personal religion which he developed for himself under the impact of nineteenth-century vitalism is as hard to define in positive terms as the religion of Meredith's English master, Thomas Carlyle. In Meredith's ethical system there are several cardinal vices, all of which are "lesser included offenses" comprehended under a single term. The first of these vices is asceticism.

Asceticism: Asceticism is typified in Meredith's work by Lord Fleetwood, the husband of Carinthia in *The Amazing Marriage* - the richest peer in England, a man of complete honor according to the conventional code of honor, and a man who makes a fatal mistake when he marries and then spurns his wife, whom he realizes too late is the woman who could have saved him. He becomes a monk, Brother Russett, and "perished of his own austerities." This denial of the body was entirely futile and destructive from Meredith's point of view, which has led his detractors to call him a "pagan" author, and his supporters to consider him "realistic" in his approach to the question.

Sensualism: The opposite vice is sensualism - one may remember his phrase in *Diana of the Crossways* about "the ascetic rocks and the sensual whirlpool." Sensualism, or the unrestrained and undisciplined submission to man's animality, is equally as bad as asceticism for Meredith. *In The Ordeal of*

Richard Feverel, Sir Austin Feverel has strong elements of asceticism in his nature, as did Meredith himself for a time after the disastrous ending of his first marriage. Adrian Harley is a discreet sensualist, on the other hand.

Sentimentalism: The ascetic and the sensualist are at least comparatively easy to identify. The sentimentalist is more elusive, and more dangerous for this reason. A reading of the *Essay on Comedy* will convince one that Meredith thought ill of the sentimentalist. Sentimentalists are snobs in the spiritual world. A concentration on snobbery in a material sense forms much of the burden of *Evan Harrington* - the question of the nature of the gentleman, and whether the traits of gentility are innate or acquired. A snob in the material or social world evaluates himself in terms of a pretended superiority in rank, wealth, or family connections. This snobbery is a fairly obvious trait - witness Lord Laxley, in *Evan Harrington*. But the sentimentalist who congratulates himself that he is possessed of finer feelings than the run of mankind is an extremely dangerous person. Sir Willoughby Patterne is a sentimentalist; so is Sir Austin Feverel. "The sentimental people," wrote Diana, "fiddle harmonics on the strings of sensualism." That is, they deceive themselves as to the animal basis of their feelings. Sir Willoughby is full of concern for his intended bride, as is Sir Austin Feverel for his son. "Not I as commoner men," these people say. Brute selfishness masquerading as fine feeling and sincere concern for the welfare of others is a very hard thing to guard against.

Egoism: But the vices of asceticism, sensualism, and sentimentalism are all comprehended by the term "egoism," which is the cardinal sin in the Meredithian ethic; it assumes the same importance to Meredith that spiritual pride and hardness of heart had for Hawthorne. In the "Introduction" to *The Egoist*, Meredith writes: "Now the world is possessed of a certain big book, the biggest book on earth; that might indeed be called the *Book of Earth*; whose title is *The Book of Egoism*."

Why, then, did Meredith dwell so much upon egoism and its subsidiary vices throughout his work? For answer to this central question, let us turn to an explication of *The Thrush in February*.

Analysis Of *The Thrush In February*: We may pass quickly over the first dozen or so stanzas, while commenting that this use of the symbol of the thrush is a characteristic device of Meredith. An ethical idea is conveyed under the aspect of a natural image. This is a fundamental Meredithian device, and it is used in his fiction also, as one may see from a reading of *The Ordeal of Richard Feverel*. The thrush is

A herald of the million bills.

In another Meredith poem, *The Lark Ascending* (1881), we see this same symbol

In whom the millions rejoice
For giving their one spirit voice

in the shape of the lark. And the object symbolized in both cases is the Meredithian hero; the poet-prophet who is to lead the race in the direction of perfection. It has been said that Thomas Carlyle was Meredith's master among English writers. One of Carlyle's chief ideas concerned the nature of the Hero - the supremely able, almost godlike, man, who could guide his fellows along "the way where they should go." We will distinguish between Meredith's and Carlyle's conception of the hero later, but for the moment one may equate the thrush in this poem with the prophetic voice of the Hero who adumbrates the man of the future, without any reference to the scientific and philosophical background out of which these ideas arose.

In the **stanzas** beginning at line 45, the **protagonist** of *The Thrush in February*, who may be taken as Meredith himself, is passing from quiescence to strenuous life as the spring succeeds the winter.

> **Imbedded in a land of greed,**
> **Of mammon-quakings dire as Earth's,**
> **My care was but to soothe my need;**
> **At peace among the little worths.**

Here we observe Meredith's compression of phrase, in a dramatic statement which does not really tell the truth. One would think that the Meredith persona is isolated in a hostile society: the conception of the artist we have come to expect in twentieth-century society. But this view is demolished by what follows, in lines 59–60:

> **I keep the youth of souls who pitch**
> **Their joy in this old heart of things.**

This exuberance and social purpose in the face of "a land of greed" may be unappealing to the modern reader nurtured on Joyce, Pound, and Eliot; but we are not attempting a value-judgment on Meredith's ethical system; we are looking rather for an understanding of its basic points.

Spring - "the Coming" - is the regeneration of earth by the agency of Nature. The "Coming" has a messianic **connotation** which Meredith probably wished it to have, for it is one of his characteristics that he sometimes employs the language of orthodox religion, while giving the meanings a twist so that read against the background of his ethical teachings, the poems are far removed from any known brand of Christianity.

> **Full lasting is the song, though he,**
> **The singer passes: lasting too,**
> **For souls not lent in usury,**
> **The rapture of the forward view.**
>
> **Nought else are we when sailing brave**
> **Save husks to raise and bid it burn.**
> **Glimpse of its livingness will wave**
> **A light the senses can discern**
>
> **Across the river of death**
> **Their close....**

Immortality: Does this posit a personal immortality? Hardly. For Meredith it was our positive thoughts and deeds which were everlasting in their effects in this world, the only world we can know. In Memoriam Tennyson agonized over the question of personal survival, personal immortality. Meredith pays very little attention to the concept.

> **I hear, I would the City heard.**
> **The City of the smoky fray;**
> **A prodded ox, it drags and moans:**
> **Its Morrow no man's child; its Day**
> **A vulture's morsel beaked to bones.**
>
> **It strikes without a mark for strife;**
> **It feasts beside a famished host:**
>
> **The loose restraint of wanton life**
> **That threatened penance in the ghost.**

The last two lines of the above **stanza** are a contemptuous reference to orthodox Christianity which, by focusing man's attention away from nature and toward a supernatural life, was in his view inhibiting the progress of the race by catering to man's irrational fears. The City as an image is no exaggeration, for in the industrial cities that were growing up during the Victorian era there was, in the eyes of thoughtful writers of the persuasion of Carlye and Meredith, truly a striving "without a mark for strife," or a purposeless struggle with material objects. And the only consolation of the City is a poor one: the moribund supernatural elements of "revealed" religion which had been eroded by new geological information, by the Higher Criticism of the Bible, and most important by the theory of evolution as summarized and focused by Darwin.

The Hero: The Meredithian Hero, then, is attracted to the City while knowing full well the magnitude of his task. The Hero is the "warrior of the sighting brain." The City represents the purposeless acquisitive and commercial instinct, which the Hero will direct into channels that will lead the race upward to "certain nobler races, now only dimly imagined," as the Meredithian phrase is in his novel, *Diana of the Crossways*. Despite the hardness of the struggle, the Heroes are drawn to it. This is not merely the expression of a gushing and vapid philosophy of service; it is based on a definite, though unsystematic **metaphysical** view of man's place in the universe. Meredith was no more a systematic philosopher than was Carlyle, but he, like Carlyle, based his ethics upon his **metaphysical** theory.

"The tidal multitude and blind," then, are to be led by the Hero "from bestial to the higher breed." Notice the emphasis on struggle and conflict all through this poem. Under the impact of evolutionary thought, life was conceived of as a severely competitive struggle, and in this, more than almost anything else in the ethical realm, the nineteenth century differed from, say, the twelfth. In the ages of faith, salvation was open to all, and was not a competitive good which, statistically, could be obtained by few.

"In His will is our peace," said Piccarda in the third Canto of the *Paradiso*, and this cardinal statement of the Dantean worldview is dead against the idea of competitive evolution. God is the goal to which all things tend, and the place appointed for an individual soul, once reached, its highest good is to occupy that place throughout eternity in the glorification of God. But the final end of competitive evolution is something quite different for the nineteenth-century writers, and for Meredith there is no final end, there is only a direction.

In line 100 we find the first reference to the supreme power of love in the Meredithian ethic. It is love that is the "crowning sun" for Meredith, as we may see in the key poem, XXX, of *Modern Love*, and in every one of Meredith's novels. The right relation of the sexes is the most important of Meredith's meanings for the word, although he uses it in a wider sense of Nature through an understanding of her purposive quality. *Modern Love* is the verse narrative of love gone wrong and of its fatal consequences for the individual and for society. *The Ordeal of Richard Feverel* is another account of the wrong kind of love based on the essentially selfish and egoistic outlook of Sir Austin Feverel. Both of these works stem from an aspect of Meredith's personal history not touched on at all in *Evan Harrington*, and which is important as background for his preoccupation with the social process of finding a suitable mate which appears in every Meredith novel.

But the mating process has implications far beyond the merely personal, for it is through the right attitude to and use of it that the race will evolve to higher things. It does not involve a merely physical reproduction; it is concerned with the refinement of thought and feeling which has led us "from slimy rock."

> **They scorned the ventral dream of peace**
> **Unknown in nature. This they knew:**
> **That life begets with fair increase**
> **Beyond the flesh, if life be true.**

In these lines (101–104) he sets up an opposition between the merely physical view of life and the evolution of flesh into spirit. The "ventral dream of peace" is animalism yet unknown even among the animals. "They," who properly scorned this dream, are the Heroes, types of the future men who will be as Gods. Personal immortality is not implied when he writes

> **That life begets with fair increase**
> **Beyond the flesh, if life be true.**

"True" does not imply Christian salvation, but evolutionary progress through work, discipline of self, and the right view of nature and love.

> **Just reason based on valiant blood**
> **The instinct bred afield would match**
> **To pipe thereof a swelling flood,**
> **Were men of Earth made wide in watch.**

Trevelyan glosses this passage as follows: "If modern men would patiently learn the secret of Earth, their intellect, based on courage, would match the primitive instincts, and so raise a swelling flood of song." And he is right insofar as he finds that Meredith is not trying to escape the "primitive instincts," but rather to use them as a basis for the development of "brain," and out of the two together, "spirit."

If this sounds an optimistic rose-pink view of existence, such an interpretation does not do justice to the **realism** of Meredith. He is aware of the terrible hardness of life. "In youth I looked out from under a hail of blows," he said, and he was not exaggerating even though he did not live in utter poverty. His marriage to Mary Ellen Peacock was a disaster, and it does great honor to Meredith's character that he was able to recover from it. He was not innocent of blame in the **catastrophe**, as he revealed in *Modern Love* and in *The Ordeal of Richard Feverel*. A terrible blow to his pride must have occurred when his wife ran off with the painter Henry Wallis in the summer of 1857 and bore a son by Wallis in 1858; a child which was Meredith's according to the law. All this, Meredith takes into account, and if one wishes to evaluate an author in terms of life-history and its relation to his work, Meredith certainly had less to be optimistic about than Robert Browning - which makes the development of his optimism all the more remarkable.

The Hero is referred to when Meredith says

Though now the numbers count as drops
An urn might bear, they father Time.
She shapes anew her dusty crops;
Her quick in their own likeness climb. (112)

The Hero represents the wave of the future, yet he is ever rooted in Nature, which is what is meant when Meredith says

They climb to light, in her their root. (114)

Evolution: Man evolves out of Nature, Spirit out of Blood and Brain in the triad which Meredith sets up in *The Woods of Westermain*. To attempt to escape physical nature is asceticism for Meredith; it contributes nothing to race progress and deserves the whips of the Comic Spirit rather than praise for holiness.

> **A slayer, yea, as when she pressed**
> **Her savage to the slaughter-heaps,**
> **To sacrifice she prompts her best:**
> **She reaps them as the sower reaps.**
>
> **But read her thought to speed the race,**
> **And stars rush forth of blackest night:**
> **You chill not at a cold embrace**
> **To come, nor dread a dubious might.**

Here Meredith is speaking as the Poet-Prophet about the illusory nature of suffering. As the evolutionists taught, life is a desperate struggle, and the unfit are weeded out by the process of natural selection. This is not perceived by those who utter the "brutish cry at muffled fate." Meredith is not saying that this is the best of all possible worlds, for it is still in the process of evolving toward some goal now only "dimly imagined." Men have evolved out of savagery through struggle, and it is largely because of the heroism of "fighting souls of love divined" that they have progressed even this far.

> **Her double visage, double voice,**
> **In oneness rise to quench the doubt.**
> **This breath, her gift, has only choice of service**
> **Breathe we in or out.**

> Since Pain and Pleasure on each hand
> Led our wild steps from slimy rock
> To yonder sweeps of gardenland,
> We breathe but to be sword or block.

One may connect this statement with obiter dicta of Diana. It will be remembered that one of Meredith's unique techniques was his use of a mythical book of maxims or sayings interpolated into his novels; sayings which explain the action and in a way modify it. The most famous of these is, of course, "The Pilgrim's Scrip," in *The Ordeal of Richard Feverel*. In *The Amazing Marriage*, Captain Kirby, the Old Buccaneer, writes his "Maxims for Men." And in *Diana of the Crossways* we find Diana's aphorisms inscribed in the "Leaves from the Diary of Henry Wilmers." One is never certain whether these sayings reflect the opinion of Meredith himself, for they are uttered dramatically; but in some cases we can have a pretty good idea that the author himself is speaking. Diana wrote and this key quotation bears repeating:

> **A brown cone drops from the fir-tree below my window, a nibbled green from the squirrel. Service is our destiny in life or in death. Then let it be my choice living to serve the living, and be fretted uncomplainingly. If I can assure myself of doing service I have my home within.**

This expresses the same thought as we find in the **stanzas** just quoted from *The Thrush in February*, the absolute equation of man with Nature. There is no dualism in Meredith's philosophy; no mortal antipathy between man and Nature, or between Flesh and Spirit. Tennyson had posed this same agonizing question for the Victorians some thirty-five years earlier in In Memoriam, of which we may cite the two most significant sections for this matter:

LV

The wish, that of the living whole
  No life may fail beyond the grave,
  Derives it not from what we have
The likest God within the soul?

Are God and Nature then at strife,
  That Nature lends such evil dreams?
  So careful of the type she seems,
So careless of the single life,

That I, considering everywhere
  Her secret meaning in her deeds,
  And finding that of fifty seeds
She often brings but one to bear,

I falter where I firmly trod,
  And falling with my weight of cares
  Upon the great world's alter-stairs
That slope thro' darkness up to God,

I stretch lame hands of faith, and grope,
  And gather dust and chaff, and call
  To what I feel is Lord of all,
And faintly trust the larger hope.

LVI

"So careful of the type?" but no.
  From scarped cliff and quarried stone She cries,
  "A thousand types are gone;
I care for nothing, all shall go.

"Thou makest thine appeal to me.
  I bring to life, I bring to death;
  The spirit does but mean the breath:
I know no more." And he, shall he,

Man, her last work, who seem'd so fair,
  Such splendid purpose in his eyes,
  Who roll'd the psalm to wintry skies,
Who built him fanes of fruitless prayer,

Who trusted God was love indeed
  And love Creation's final law -
  Tho' Nature, red in tooth and claw
With ravine, shriek'd against his creed -

Who loved, who suffer'd countless ills,
  Who battled for the True, the Just,
  Be blown about the desert dust,
Or seal'd within the iron hills?

No more? A monster then, a dream,
  A discord. Dragons of the prime,
  That tare each other in their slime,
Were mellow music match'd with him.

O life as futile, then, as frail!
  O for thy voice to soothe and bless!
  What hope of answer, or redress?
Behind the veil, behind the veil.

This is the converse of the position taken by Meredith in *The Thrush in February* and throughout his work. It is, of course, a dramatic statement by the persona of In Memoriam, who may only roughly be equated with the poet. A dualism is established between Man and Nature; Nature who is pitiless and indifferent; the "Everlasting No" of Sartor Resartus. And ever since, the prevailing view of Nature has been tending toward, say, Hardy's or Robinson Jeffers', and away from Meredith's.

What Meredith means by his anti-dualistic view is this: human life originates in Nature, or Earth, and out of Earth, which is sometimes referred to as "Blood," evolves Brain, or intelligence. But Brain is built upon the lower faculty, and must include it. Blood and Brain together evolve Spirit, when "intelligence and instinct" become one. This evolutionary process comes only through intense and brutal struggle, and if the individual does not read aright the "letters on Nature's breast" he will be destroyed, and worse, may drag down entirely innocent people with him. Man's life is equated with natural process, and this unalterable law must be accepted.

> **The sighting brain her good decree**
> **Accepts; obeys those guides, in faith,**
> **By reason hourly fed, that she,**
> **To some the clod, to some the wraith,**
>
> **Is more, no mask; a flame, a stream,**
> **Flame, stream, are we, in mid career**
> **From torrent source, delirious dream,**
> **To heaven-reflecting currents clear.**

"Her good decree" as interpreted by Meredith, involves complete acceptance of "her thoughts to speed the race," and a participation in the struggle of evolution. Love is the chief crown of this struggle.

The last **stanza** of *The Thrush in February* will serve to throw some light on the terribly tragic ending of *The Ordeal of Richard Feverel*. Note that there is still no hint of personal immortality.

Man's physical death must be accepted as a part of the processes of nature:

> **When lowly, with a broken neck,**
> **The crocus lays her cheek to mire.**

It conforms to physical laws, and argument with these laws is futile, and is based on a wrong conception of nature.

Lucifer In Starlight: *Lucifer in Starlight* develops this **theme** of natural law; it is a fairly well-known **sonnet**, which has often been misread. "Sinners hugged their specter of repose." The question is, sinners against what? And what is it that Lucifer revolted against in his "old revolt from Awe?" True, Meredith is using Christian terminology here, but in the light of the evolutionary view of nature which we know he held, the Christian terms must be taken to stand for something else. Lucifer's sin was pride, an instant of rebellion against the will of God. Translated into Meredithian terms, Lucifer is the chaotic principle in the universe, the anti-evolutionary principle. Lucifer in Meredithian terms, personifies all those egotistic elements in man's nature which place him in isolation from the current of evolution and of devout acceptance of the scheme of things. "The army of unalterable law" is the physical law of evolution, as given an ethical turn by Meredith. If Meredith has a "God" in his system, it must be the impersonal laws of the conservation of matter and the conservation of energy, which were beginning to be understood in nineteenth-century physical thought. The total quantity of matter in the universe is a constant. "Change is on the wing to bud/ Rose in brain from rose in blood." Change is the law of life, yet, under it all, although everything changes, nothing dies. The stars in this **sonnet**, "the brain of heaven," personify or represent the physical laws which govern the universe; and if there is a God, it is the force which has established these laws.

But it is not man's place to ask questions. In the poem, *The Question Whither*, (1888), Meredith said:

> **Then let our trust be firm in Good,**
>   **Though we be of the fasting;**
> **Our questions are a mortal brood,**
>   **Our work is everlasting.**
> **We children of Beneficence**
>   **Are in its being sharers;**
> **And Whither vainer sounds than Whence,**
>   **For word with such wayfarers.**

Meredith's novels have never enjoyed a huge popular success, and his poetry has been largely ignored. This is not due solely to its obscurity; it is rather because his temper has been diametrically opposed to the present spirit of the age.

Meredith's long philosophical poem, *The Woods of Westermain* (1883), is a full expression of the evolutionary struggle and the need for its acceptance by man, as well as of the oneness of man and nature. The short poem, *Woodland Peace* (1870), may be taken as a *Woods of Westermain* in miniature.

> **Here all say,**
> **We serve her, even as I:**
> **We brood, we strive to sky,**
> **We gaze upon decay,**
> **We wot of life through death,**
> **How each feeds each we spy;**
> **And is a tangle round,**
> **Are patient; what is dumb We question not, nor ask**
> **The silent to give sound,**
> **The hidden to unmask,**
> **The distant to draw near.**

Meredith's Critique Of Religious Orthodoxy: Again we find the temper of the poem to be against vain theological questionings. It will be helpful to recall a comment which Carlyle made, in Past and Present, about nineteenth-century Methodism:

> **Methodism, with its eye forever turned on its own navel; asking itself with torturing anxiety of Hope and Fear, "Am I right? am I wrong? shall I be saved? shall I not be damned?"-what is this, at bottom, but a new phasis of Egoism, stretched out into the Infinite not always the heavenlier for its infinitude.**

Preoccupation with personal salvation and survival after death seemed unworthy for both Carlyle and Meredith. Carlyle, writing earlier, did not come as much under the influence of the evolutionists. He believed, and he preached in Sartor Resartus and elsewhere, that in Nature, everything has a "place" assigned it, ranging from mere Chaos at the very bottom up to God, or "The One; Pure Form, Substance, and Actuality." Yet this does not imply a machine-universe, for the universe is evolving from chaos toward greater form and organization. Society is a microcosm of the whole universe, in which there must be due subordination, but which should be based on ability and innate qualities of character, and not on "clothes." The natural leaders of man, like Abbot Samson in Past and Present, will lead him in the struggle to bring order out of chaos by useful work. (The final message of Carlyle, in Sartor Resartus and elsewhere, may be summed up in the lines from "The Everlasting Yea": "Work while it is called Today; for the Night cometh, wherein no man can work." Concern with one's own paltry salvation is egoism, for both Carlyle and Meredith.

Carlyle's attitude toward these matters was essentially religious; it was based on the same sort of intuition or faith upon which, say, the religion of John Henry Newman rested. Meredith, while he held much the same views as Carlyle concerning the place of man in Nature, the function of the Hero, the organizing principle of society, and the necessity of struggle and work to bring order out of chaos and lead man to higher forms of existence - Meredith had a scientific theory which lent support to this view. It is a mistake to say that he and his contemporaries had their faith shattered all at once with the appearance of *The Origin of Species* in 1859. The Higher Criticism of the Bible, a factor completely unrelated to the development of scientific evolutionary thought, had been at work well in advance of the promulgation of Darwinism and had undercut the position of orthodox Christianity. David Friedrich Strauss wrote in the Preface to *The Life of Jesus* (1835; tr. by George Eliot, 1846), the following interesting observation:

> **The author is aware that the essence of the Christian faith is perfectly independent of his criticism. The supernatural birth of Christ, his miracles, his resurrection and ascension, remain eternal truths, whatever doubts may be cast on their reality as historical facts. The certainty of this can alone give calmness and dignity to our criticism, and distinguish it from the naturalistic criticism of the last century, the design of which was, with the historical fact, to subvert also the religious truth, and which thus necessarily became frivolous. A dissertation at the close of the work will show that the dogmatic significance of the life of Jesus remains inviolate: in the meantime let the calmness and insensibility with which, in the course of it, criticism undertakes apparently dangerous operations, be explained solely by the security of the author's conviction that no injury is threatened to the Christian faith.**

Into the intellectual and religious atmosphere thus created by the questioning of the mysteries of Faith, the idea of evolution through natural selection came with terrific impact. The special creation of man; his state of innocence before the Fall and his chance for salvation, were replaced by an inconceivably long natural process which questioned the Biblical account of creation and the length of time which had elapsed for man to exist. How could man have an immortal soul destined for future reward and punishment if he was only a more highly organized animal? These issues are commonplaces now, and there is scarcely any serious discussion of them

Nature: The most shocking thing to the Victorians about the theory of evolution was not its calling into question of the teachings of "revealed" religion and the historical authenticity of the Bible. This had already been questioned - at a time much earlier than the period under discussion - during the Enlightenment, as the study of what we would call today comparative religion arose on the Continent, in the writings of the French Encyclopedists. But evolution presented a bleak picture of Nature; one far from that held by the Romantic poets, especially Wordsworth; a Nature indifferent if not actively hostile to man; a Nature where struggle was the law of existence, where, as Hardy put it in *Jude the Obscure*: "Nature's law...is mutual butchery." The conclusions to which this view of Nature led have been examined in some detail by Professor Joseph Warren Beach in *The Concept of Nature in Nineteenth-Century English Poetry*. In general, Tennyson and Arnold were led to negative conclusions, as was Hardy, and Edward Fitzgerald, the translator of the Rubaiyat. Browning retained an optimism and a belief in the goodness of man's spiritual goal.

"On the earth the broken arcs; in the heaven a perfect round." But Meredith is the most uncompromising in his optimism and his acceptance of the evolutionary struggle. Only Swinburne approaches him in this matter; Swinburne, who in the *Hymn of Man* (1871) and in *Hertha* (1871) revealed his view of the oneness of man and nature and of the possibility of man's growth to higher things:

> **I the grain and the furrow,**
>   **The plow-cloven clod**
> **And the plowshare drawn thorough,**
>   **The germ and the sod,**
> **The deed and the doer, the seed and the**
>   **sower, the dust which is God.**

Meredith did not "anticipate" the evolutionary theory, but when it was promulgated, he took it up at once and made it his own. When he entered the Moravian school at Neuwied on the Rhine at age 14 (1842), he was exposed to a liberal intellectual and religious atmosphere, and, as he says, to Niebuhr - pioneer of the evolutionary view of history, who stressed ethnological distinctions, institutions, tendencies, and social traits to the neglect of individuals - and to Goethe, whom he termed "the most enduring." From these two German sources he could easily have derived the general concept of development.

He went through a six-week conversion experience and never thereafter "swallowed the Christian fable." Thereafter, he developed his own private ethical system.

Lionel Stevenson, in his book, *Darwin Among the Poets*, sets up a contrast between Meredith and Browning which would be valuable to consider. He writes:

> **In defining Meredith's interpretation of the evolutionary idea, it will be profitable to compare**

him with Browning. Between the conclusions of the two poets regarding the conduct of life there is a close similarity, but in the arguments from which the conclusions were drawn there is wide divergence. Both, although discounting the notion of any sudden improvement in mankind, yet held the chief sin to be indolent evasion of vigorous effort, and counseled for every man perpetual and cheerful struggle toward his ideal. Both were confident that the trend of such conflict is toward ultimate perfection. But the two assumptions on which Browning based all his theory - the validity of the Christian creed and the immortality of the individual soul - were the very things which Meredith most vehemently denied.

"We live in what we have done," Meredith wrote in one of his letters, and this remark is amplified by his poem, *A Faith on Trial* (1888), which commemorated the death of his second wife, and may be taken as the Meredithan *In Memoriam*. His wife, with whom his marriage had been as happy as his first marriage had been bitter, died in September, 1885. Nature - the earth, in answer to man's craving for personal immortality, which Meredith interpreted as egoism, answers in this poem as the

> Mother of simple truth,
> Relentless quencher of lies;
> Eternal in thought; discerned
> In thought mid-ferry between
> The Life and the Death, which are one,
> As our breath in or out, joy or teen.

Of the dead, Tennyson wrote in *In Memoriam*: that they are "brothers of an ampler day." In some way, personal immortality is a reality. In contrast to this, Meredith said:

> These men live in us. And more, they are the higher work of Nature, which she will not let pass away. They have the eternal in them. I do not look on death as a victory over us. Death and life are neighbors, each the cause of the other....

This letter may be taken as a gloss on the poem *A **Ballad** of past Meridian*. In this poem, Death simply says "I gather." Remember the lines in *The Thrush in February*:

> Life was to them the bag of grain,
> And Death the weedy harrow's tooth.

No promise of personal immortality is made. In the second **stanza**, Life is presented in all its hardness: "how naked and how hard when known!"

The key line is the last one: "Of Death, of Life, those inwound notes are mine." Death and Life are aspects of natural process which, if rightly considered, and if one lives in conformity with nature's laws, leads to the development of "certain nobler races, now very dimly imagined."

Relevance Of Meredith's Personal Life: Meredith had two great personal tragedies. The first was his marriage with the widowed Mary Ellen Nicolls, and its disastrous failure; the second, the death of Marie Vulliamy Meredith in 1885. *Modern Love*, his first great poem, is the record of the first marriage. The one **sonnet**, or poem (as the 50 poems of *Modern Love* contain sixteen lines each), which we have included in this discussion is, in all probability, the one poem which may be taken as the key to the sequence. The first eight lines may be taken as a straight Meredithian utterance on the trinity of Blood, Brain, and Spirit. Spirit evolves only when "intelligence and instinct now are one."

The explication of the last half of the poem is more difficult if we treat it in isolation from the entire sequence, as we must. In the sequence, there are two women: "Madam," the poet's wife, and "my Lady," who is his mistress. In the last eight lines, which are very difficult if taken "straight," the poet is mocking himself. The principals of the poem stand for Meredith and his first wife. They are - to take the title of a later Meredithian novel which recounted a similar disastrous love - relation ending in the death of the hero - "tragic comedians." The speaker is not free from guilt in the poem, and he recognizes this. He is equally responsible for the tragedy with the woman. The last eight lines of poem XXX, then are an ironic statement, based on the experience of the **protagonist** of the poem.

Conclusion: What, then, can we conclude about Meredith on the basis of the examination of these few poems? It is that Meredith's ideas are relatively few and clear-cut, and that as an artist he is significant for the number of and variety of his illustrations of these ideas in the Victorian period. In the novels he embodied the evolutionary struggle, the Hero in the service of humanity, the relationship of the sexes - he presented both a "norm," and a departure from this norm dramatically. In his poetry there is less of the dramatic (*Modern Love* is a significant exception), and more direct statement, but it never becomes mere versified preaching. Meredith's poetic imagination, which operated in an essentially **Metaphysical** manner, was too strong for the writing of jingling **didactic** verse, although at his worst Meredith's poetry is banal and thin. Meredith took over the theory of competitive evolution and gave it an ethical turn. Darwin, in *The Origin of Species*, had no such intention. At the conclusion of the *Origin of Species*, it is true, Darwin cautiously spoke of Creation in these terms, and it is worthwhile to include his summary as an illustration of the laws he was attempting to state:

> It is interesting to contemplate a tangled bank, clothed with many plants of many kinds, with birds singing on the bushes, with various insects flitting about, and with worms crawling through the damp earth, and to reflect that these elaborately constructed forms, so different from each other, and dependent upon each other in so complex a manner, have all been produced by laws acting around us. These laws, taken in the largest sense, being Growth with Reproduction; Inheritance which is almost implied by reproduction; Variability from the indirect and direct action of the conditions of life, and from use and disuse: a Ratio of Increase so high as to lead to a Struggle for Life, and as a consequence to Natural Selection, entailing Divergence of Character and the Extinction of less-improved forms. Thus, from the war of nature, from famine and death, the most exalted object which we are capable of conceiving, namely, the production of the higher animals, directly follows.

Meredith, seizing upon these hypotheses, made of them a religion. He was a poet, and passed far beyond the range of science in his language. What exactly was the spiritual element which he saw in Nature? This is at the heart of any consideration of Meredith's poetry. The spiritual element was simply that which man was evolving. Just what man was evolving toward is not clear. Spirit raves not for a goal," wrote Meredith. Evolution is a direction, but there is no "far-off Divine Event" implied, no consummation of the world. Before man was sentient, there was no spiritual element present in Nature.

Is there a teleological view of nature in Meredith's writing? In terms of final ends, no. As Professor Beach writes, however, of the Meredithian ethic :

> **It is possible for men of cultivated imagination to conceive of themselves as part of a life-process which moves in the direction of spirituality, and to sink their personal pains and failures in a sense of the larger life of .which they are a part. Some other thinker, with all the same facts in mind, might easily reply: The pains and failures involved in the total life process so greatly outweigh the spiritual gratifications as to make them virtually negligible.**

In the last analysis, then, we have a question of faith and of temperament. The validity of Meredith's ethic is no more capable of scientific proof than is Hardy's or Browning's or Swinburne's views of existence.

In 1876 Meredith said that the following four lines, which appear in the novel *Vittoria* (1866), were his favorite passage from his poetry:

> **Our life is but a little holding, lent**
> **To do a mighty labour: we are one**
> **With heaven and the stars when it is spent**
> **To serve God's aim: else die we with the sun.**

In the highly elliptical language which Meredith's poetry employs, the only God present here is the law of the conservation of matter and the conservation of energy. Everything changes; the Singer passes, but the song remains. Meredith was consistent to the last; he was not a trimmer, except about social status. The verse is graven upon his tomb.

The individual soul passes, but its work survives if it has obeyed the law of nature, in harmony with the rest of the physical universe, and if it has labored confidently toward the vision of future progress. One might think from this **exposition** that the individual has no chance to do anything constructive, bound as he is by the laws of the physical universe. But Meredith held that the individual could, by his conscious effort, hasten the progress of evolution. All the Meredithian vices, and especially egoism, are retarders of evolution, and could destroy both the individual and the race. Success or failure in reading aright the laws of nature and in bringing oneself into conformity with these laws to "speed the race" or hinder it - this is the basis of the Meredithian novel.

THE ORDEAL OF RICHARD FEVEREL

CRITICAL COMMENTARY

The approach to this novel has been established in the chapters dealing, respectively, with the novel of philosophical **satire** and with the relation of Meredith's poetry to his fiction; this includes comments from some of the leading critics of Meredith, and it would be superfluous to repeat them here.

However, the study of scholarship and criticism on Meredith is interesting. A student who consults the annotated Bibliography below will note that there was a long period after the novelist's death in which there was little writing being done concerning his work, and this is in contrast to the interest in such other Victorian novelists as Hardy (especially), Dickens, Thackeray, and the Brontes. The explanation of this is that, in the first place, Meredith, as Henry James, is difficult to understand. His language is subtle, and even more mannered than that of James. Further, in many ways, he was primarily a poet. *The Ordel of Richard Feverel* is one of the most poetic novels in English, and the characteristics of poetry - compression, **imagery**, symbolism, obliqueness of language, even rhythm - do not always make for clarity, nor should they.

Beyond these merely surface difficulties with Meredith, readers have had another and more fundamental difficulty: Meredith's evident and bracing optimism in the face of the hardness of modern life. It may be remembered that one of Meredith's chief admirers, the late and great English historian, George Macaulay Trevelyan, thought of the poet and novelist as actualizing and embodying the very genius of English institutions; the only book, indeed, the only study, of much value on Meredith's poetry is that of Trevelyan, written a half-century ago.

But in the interval there have been two disastrous World Wars, and the public temper does not take kindly to such optimism, or fancied optimism, as is perceived in Meredith. For Meredith to seem to imply that there is a redeeming feature, in non-Christian terms, in such unbearable and tragic incidents as the death of Lucy, has not gone down well, and his readership has shrunk proportionately. However, an author such as Hardy, since he was both poet and novelist, in many ways serves to contrast admirably with Meredith in this respect; Hardy has been more admired in our century because in his pessimistic determinism and naturalism, coupled with a true tragic vision, he has seemed to be more descriptive of actuality than has Meredith.

It was after the Second World War that a kind of revival of interest in Meredith's fiction took place, the post-World War I temper being strongly against him. Today many of his novels are in print and in widely-circulated paperback editions; this is especially true of *The Ordeal of Richard Feverel*, which is undoubtedly his most popular novel as well as one of his most distinguished works, because Meredith tended to repeat himself in his later novels. As the critic E. A. Baker said, "Meredith had become Meredithian" in such works as *Celt and Saxon* and *The Amazing Marriage*.

In his confronting of the facts of man's suffering and death, in his analysis of human love and sexuality, and in his incorporation into his philosophy of the teachings of his contemporary science, Meredith was certainly in advance of his time. Without being obvious about it, he turned his back on all religion that made any claim to special knowledge or supernatural revelation - he is clearer about his position in the poetry than he is in his fiction. The **conventions** of Victorianism were flouted by Meredith, but not obviously; he could not be frank and be published, so he became hyper-sophisticated in his treatment of character, situation, and dialogue, and thus got away with more than any of his contemporaries. This is not to say that he did so from any corrupt motive; he was not prurient - quite the reverse. It can be surmised that if he had written more plainly, *The Ordeal of Richard Feverel* would not have been published at all.

What has perhaps not been sufficiently perceived is that Meredith, at least in *The Ordeal of Richard Feverel*, became a writer of truly tragic stature. The final **catastrophe**, with the death of the innocent, can be ranked with the tragedies of Aeschylus, Sophocles, Euripides - or Shakespeare.

The reader of *The Ordeal of Richard Feverel* would do well simply to read the novel, carefully and with close attention to the interplay of language and situation and to the obliqueness of Meredith's implicational diction. The secondary sources listed in the Bibliography, and with notes on particular points may be consulted, but the primary emphasis is on the texts, and, as the thesis of this Guide to Meredith has been all along, the basis of Meredith's philosophy of the novel is to be found in his poetry and in his *Essay on Comedy*.

THE ORDEAL OF RICHARD FEVEREL

ESSAY QUESTIONS AND ANSWERS

Question: What is the purpose and nature of Sir Austin Feverel's System?

Answer: Sir Austin, as a result of his own unhappy experience with his wife, who had deserted him in favor of the weak and irresponsible Denzil Somers, decides that, while it is necessary for Richard to marry eventually, in order to provide continuity in the family inheritance, he should marry only when he is thirty or older and that, even then, the marriage should be an arranged one; arranged on scientific principles, with the choice of the young lady concerned being made by Sir Austin rather than by Richard. Women, in Sir Austin's view, are the ordeal of all of the Feverels. The System of upbringing of Richard is a repressive one, and while it is calculated to make him lead his life in accordance with reason and virtue, ends up by having an effect radically different from what Sir Austin expects.

In Meredith's view, in the triad of blood, brain, and spirit, which he speaks of most directly in his poetry, Sir Austin ignores blood, even though it is the basic element out of which the other two higher faculties of mankind will grow. If the blood is denied by an unreal and repressive system, the development of the individual on the higher levels is warped and stunted. Richard turns out as well as he does not because of the System, but in spite of it. Yet, even at the disastrous end of the story of Richard and Lucy, Sir Austin still believes that he has done right, and that Richard got into difficulties as a result of disregarding his father's advice and System. In this, Sir Austin is profoundly self-deceived, and Meredith's evaluation of him is really that Sir Austin deserves what might be described as the non-religious equivalent of damnation - not by God, but by Nature, for his System went against nature.

Admittedly, exactly what Meredith meant by "Nature" is hard to define. It is more than likely that his definition would involve a vital or controlling principle of existence which makes for higher and higher ethical, physical, and spiritual development of the human race. Sir Austin's System is the result of egoism, the Meredithian cardinal sin; it involves asceticism, another such offense, and it is, therefore, an offense against life itself.

Question: What is meant by Meredith's "Vitalism?"

Answer: Vitalism is the doctrine that the processes of life are not explicable by the laws of physics and chemistry alone, and that life is in some part self-determined and self-determining; it is opposed to mechanism, or philosophical naturalism, in which a view of man involves determinism, the negation of free will, the notion that man is simply an animal who is bound by rigid natural laws from which he has no power to deviate; that any self-development takes place by accident, and that self-destruction or human deterioration is just as likely an outcome of existence as is self-development.

Meredith's vitalism is highly optimistic for the future of the human race. The individual's duty is thus to develop himself to the maximum, both physically and intellectually; these in turn will lead to increased spiritual development. Man is to have no thought whatsoever for what happens to him personally in this scheme of things; all he can do is practice cheerful acceptance of the will of Nature, no matter how hard that will may seem to be. Thus, in many of Meredith's works, not the least in *The Ordeal of Richard Feverel*, the ending may seem to be incredibly hard and tragic. But, as with all great tragedy, such an ending is affirmative, not negative, for it affirms the spirit of man; it is the "reaffirmation of the will to live in the face of death," as Nietzsche phrased the spirit of tragedy. Vitalism then is developmental and dynamic, and the individual's duty is to accept and to cooperate fully with the will of Nature, expressed through her laws, in human development toward "certain nobler races," as Meredith said in *Diana of the Crossways*.

Question: What is the function of Adrian Harley, "the Wise Youth?"

Answer: "Wise," of course, is an ironic description of Adrian. He is a complete hedonist, existing only for his pleasures, which he arranges with discretion. These are of a physical nature, and there are many implications and hints that Adrian has seduced various of the farm-girls in the vicinity of Raynham. Meredith regards him unsympathetically, with his wisdom being very shallow and his activities essentially destructive in terms of human progress. Anyway, Adrian is a hanger-on, whom Sir Austin uses for his own purposes as a general handyman, spy, arranger, and even fixer. Adrian attempts to detach himself from vital involvement with those around him, but his detachment is of a selfish variety, and Meredith sees him in the role of what he specifically described as the sensualist, who delights in the physical.

Sensualism, as has been pointed out in the general essays on Meredith's philosophy, is, along with asceticism, sentimentalism, and egoism, the Meredithian cardinal offense, though it is not as grave as the other three. In *The Ordeal of Richard Feverel*, Adrian Harley represents the sensualist, though this may not be readily apparent if one reads his character without some appreciation of the sophisticated nuances of his portrayal. He hides well what he is. Adrian is contrasted unfavorably with Austin Wentworth, the son of Colonel Wentworth, who is upon occasion described as almost a saint. And yet Adrian is better thought of around Raynham than is Austin, and this is a reflection of the judgment of the children of this world rather than of the children of light. The world tends to misread character, implies Meredith, drawing the contrast between Adrian and Austin, and this is no startlingly new doctrine; Meredith's artistic success lies in the subtlety with which he draws these character sketches.

Question: If Adrian represents sensualism, who represents asceticism in the novel?

Answer: Sir Austin Feverel's System is, in the last analysis, repressive to the point of asceticism, which is, of course, another of the Meredithian cardinal sins. Meredith gives us a convincing motivation for the baronet's dislike and distrust of women in that his wife had betrayed him by running away with his best friend, and brought his name into scandal in addition to deeply wounding his pride. Sir Austin then, emotionally frozen to the point where he never seems a real person, compounds his offense, which is connected with his pride and lack of acceptance of the conditions of human life, involving, as they do, suffering, and he compounds it by attempting to inflict his views on his only son.

Of course, Richard is a healthy and - despite the System - fairly sensible young man, who instinctively sees that an unnatural repression is stunting him. After being lied to by his father, by Adrian, and by many of the others who surround him, he rebels. But it is unfortunate that Sir Austin has corroboration for his ascetic System, as evidenced by the humorously disastrous interview with Ripton Thompson and the finding that Ripton is wallowing in "sinks of iniquity," because he has a few off-color magazines in his desk when he is supposed to be devoting his attention to reading the Law in a dusty office. This incident, at a crucial moment, leads Sir Austin to believe that he is absolutely on the right track in keeping Richard isolated from women, until such time as he, Sir Austin, decides he should marry and until he can choose a mate scientifically for his son. But his asceticism is self-defeating, and Sir Austin's tragedy is that he cannot, even at the end, realize this fact.

Question: What is the relation of Zoroastrianism, or the "Magian Conflict," to the **theme** of this book?

Answer: Meredith was quite interested in the Zoroastrian religion of Persia, at least as a **metaphor** or symbol, although there is no evidence that he had any belief in supernatural or revealed religion of any sort. But Meredith's father-in-law, Thomas Love Peacock, had been quite interested in Zoroastrianism. This religion, of course, is dualistic in the extreme; it posits a good Deity, Ormuzd, and an evil one, Ahriman, locked in combat. This combat is not thought to last indefinitely; one or the other force will at some distant point be permanently victorious. However, unlike the position on the warfare between God and Satan in Christian theology, there is no guarantee that it is "Good" which inevitably will be victorious. Therefore, man's duty is to cooperate with Ormuzd, or the forces of light-light being the basic symbol of Good in Zoroastrianism - in an effort to insure the victory of Good.

In *The Ordeal of Richard Feverel* there is much symbolism of a Zoroastrian sort, primarily in terms of the light-dark **imagery**. The iron-bound evidence that this was on Meredith's mind and in his artistic conception of the story is reference to such things as "the Magian conflict." Zoroaster, the Persian religious teacher, was called a "Magus," or wise man. There is a subtle interplay of such **imagery** in *The Ordeal*, climaxed in the fantastic seduction scene between Richard and the Enchantress, Bella Mount, in which the **imagery** is that of the flames of a dualistic hell.

The Ordeal, then, seems to imply a temporary triumph of evil, and this, in a complex manner, fits in with Meredith's "reading of Earth." Evil is an objective fact, whose existence must be accepted by man - but, while evil may temporarily triumph, man must reconcile himself to the destruction of his individuality, so long as the race is promoted and advanced by his efforts. "Service is our destiny, in life or in death," writes Diana, in *Diana of the Crossways*, and this is the affirmation of life which Meredith always adopted. There is, then, a distinct tie between Meredith's philosophy of nature and his use of Zoroastrianism as symbol or myth. He had, little a number of his Victorian contemporaries, but perhaps to an even greater extent, turned his back on the Christian interpretation of history, which he no longer could square with the teachings of evolutionary science, and, seeking another **metaphor** to describe the facts of existence, hit on Zoroastrianism. Nowhere in *The Ordeal of Richard Feverel* is there any serious reference to Christianity; the presentation of Lucy as a Roman Catholic is for reasons of the establishment of motivation and artistic verisimilitude. This does not mean that Meredith was anti-Christian; he was rather trying to build up a terminology by which he could best reflect reality, and this terminology happened to be Zoroastrian, for the reasons stated.

Question: How does Meredith provide sufficient motivation for Sir Austin's opposition to Richard's marriage?

Answer: The formal motivation for his intense objection is based on the prejudices of class and religion. Lucy, while her people are of the class of gentlefolk and her father had been a King's Officer in the Royal Navy and, therefore, by definition, a Gentleman, is far beneath Richard in social standing; for, as the only son and heir of a baronet, Richard is very highly placed in society. The fortune to which he is heir is substantial.

Added to the question of Richard's fortune, there is the objection which Sir Austin raises due to the religious question. As noted, Lucy's Roman Catholicism, while not made a great issue of from the point of view of theology or doctrine, has social implications that would have been strong in the rural England of the last century.

Richard is thought, by this marriage, somehow to have brought disgrace on the Feverel name in the manner of Austin Wentworth, who had married a serving-girl of bad character who had shortly left her husband. This is an unfortunate precedent also, for it has given Sir Austin a certain set of attitudes which are even stronger than he might normally have had toward such marriages. But the strongest motivation of all is simply Sir Austin's System, and his belief that he can manage Richard's life by scientific method. He cannot, but he thinks he can - and in this lie the seeds of the destruction of the innocent, which is exactly what happens in the **climax** of the novel. Sir Austin's objections are none of them rational, and Meredith implies that his pride wins out over his son's happiness.

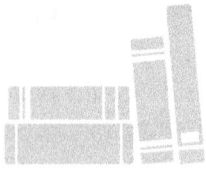

BIBLIOGRAPHY

This bibliography is divided into a general section listing a number of standard works dealing with Meredith's fiction, and a special section listing Meredith's poetry and secondary works, which comment on that poetry. The bibliography is annotated, as some of the items are considered by the author of the present study to be more useful as introductory materials than are other items.

The total amount of scholarly and critical writing concerning Meredith is not large, when comparisons are made with the amount of writing which has been done about, say, Browning, Tennyson, Dickens, Thackeray, Hardy, and Conrad, among his contemporaries. This is explained on several grounds; for one thing, Meredith has seemed obscure and difficult to many readers, and the effort of mastering his language is not justified, in this view. To this it may be answered that such a writer as James Joyce is equally as difficult, or more so - and while we are on the subject, it is interesting to observe that at a key point in *Ulysses*, Joyce has one of his characters send a telegram quoting one of Meredith's aphorisms: "A Sentimentalist is one who seeks to enjoy Reality without incurring the immense debtorship for a thing done." But while many have made the effort to understand, say, *Ulysses*, this effort has not been extended to Meredith because his philosophical outlook is rather opposed to that of a great majority of the writers of this century.

Meredith, however, both as poet and as novelist, is a writer who repays study. The "biographical fallacy" - the notion that an author's writing can be understood primarily with reference to his biography - is less invalid in the case of Meredith than in that of most other writers among his contemporaries in Victorian England. One may wish to explore some of the suggestions for further study given at the conclusion of the bibliography below.

GENERAL BIBLIOGRAPHY

Bailey, Dorothy Dee. "American Criticism of George Meredith's Novels, 1860–1895." *Transactions of the Wisconsin Academy of Sciences, Arts, and Letters*, XLVII (1958), 273–283.

Bailey, F. E. *Six Great Victorian Novelists*. London: MacDonald, 1947. [See pp. 143–169.]

Baker, Ernest A. *The History of the English Novel*. Vol. 8. From the Brontes to Meredith. London: H. F. and G. Witherby, 1937. [Chapters 7, 8, and 9 are extremely useful as an introduction to Meredith.]

Bartlett, Phyllis. *George Meredith*. London: Longmans, Green for the British Council, 1963. "Writers and Their Work, No. 161." [An important recent short introduction.]

_____."The Novels of George Meredith." *Review of English Literature* (Leeds), III (1962), 31–46.

_____."Richard Feverel: Knight-Errant," *Bulletin of the New York Public Library*, LXIII (1959), 329–340.

Beach, Joseph Warren. *The Concept of Nature in Nineteenth-Century English Poetry*. New York: Macmillan, 1936. [Important for an understanding of Meredith's ideas.]

Bennett, Arnold. *Books and Persons*. London, 1917. ["Between Fielding and Meredith no entirely honest novel was written by anybody in England. The fear of the public, the lust of popularity, feminine prudery, sentimentalism, Victorian niceness - one or other of these things prevented honesty." p. 135.]

Buchen, Irving H. "The Importance of the Minor Characters in *The Ordeal of Richard Feverel*." *Brown University Studies in English*, V (1961), 154–166.

_____."*The Ordeal of Richard Feverel* Science Versus Nature." *ELH*, XXIX (1962), 47–66.

Buckler, William E. "The Artistic Unity of Richard Feverel, Chapter XXXIII." *Nineteenth-Century Fiction*, VII (1952), 119–124.

Butcher, Lady Alice Brandreth. *Memories of George Meredith*, O. M. London: Constable, 1919. [Lady Alice was a friend of Meredith for 41 years. This book contains valuable personal reminiscences.]

Cline, C. L. "The Betrothal of George Meredith and Marie Vulliamy." *Nineteenth-Century Fiction*, XVI (1961), 231–243.

Clodd, E. "George Meredith: Some Recollections." *Fortnightly Review*, XCII (1909).

Crees, J. H. E. *George Meredith: A Study of His Works and Personality*. Oxford: Basil Blackwell, 1918.

Curtin, Frank D. "Adrian Harley: The Limits of Meredith's Comedy." *Nineteenth-Century Fiction*, VIII (1953), 272–283.

Dick, Ernst. *George Meredith*. Berlin: Weygandt and Grieben, 1910.

Ekeberg, Gladys W. "*The Ordeal of Richard Feverel* as Tragedy." *College English*, VII (1946), 387–393.

Ellis, S. M. *George Meredith: His Life and Friends in Relation to His Work.* New York: Dodd, Mead, 1920. [A standard work.]

Fanger, Donald. "George Meredith as Novelist." *Nineteenth-Century Fiction*, XVI (1962), 317–328.

Fernandez, Ramon de. "Le Message de Meredith." *Messages* (Premiere Serie), 1920.

Forman, Maurice Buxton. *A Bibliography of the Writings in Prose and Verse of George* Meredith. Edinburgh: Dunedin Press, for the Bibliographical Society, 1922.

_____.George Meredith: *Some Early Appreciations.* London: Chapman Hall, 1909. [A convenient collection of critical anecdotes.]

_____.Meredithiana: *Being a Supplement to the Bibliography of George Meredith.* Edinburgh: Dunedin Press, for the Bibliographical Society, 1924.

Galland, Rene. *George Meredith: Le Cinquante Premieres Annees, 1828–1878.* Paris: Les Presses Francaises, 1923.

Gettman, Royal A. "Serialization and Evan Harrington." *PMLA*, LXIV (1949), 963–975.

Gretton, Mary Sturge. *The Writings and Life of George Meredith: A Centenary Study.* Cambridge: Harvard University Press, 1926.

Hammerton, John A. *George Meredith: His Life and Art in Anecdote and Criticism.* Edinburgh: John Grant, 1911.

Hergenhan, L. T. "Meredith's Use of Revision: A Consideration of the Revisions of Richard Feverel and Evan Harrington." *Modern Language Review*, LIX (1964), 539–544.

_____."A Note on Some of George Meredith's Early Reviewers." *Notes and Queries*, XI (1964), 231-232.

_____."The Reception of George Meredith's Early Novels." *Nineteenth-Century Fiction*, XIX (1964), 213-235.

Hewett-Thayer, H. W. "Ferdinand Lasalle in the Novels of Spielhagen and Meredith." *Germanic Review*, XIX (1944), 186-196.

Le Gallienne, Richard. *George Meredith: Some Characteristics*. London and New York: John Lane, The Bodley Head, 1900.

Hudson, Richard B. "Meredith's Autobiography and 'The Adventures of Harry Richmond.'" *Nineteenth-Century Fiction*, IX (1954), 38-50.

Ketcham, Carl H. "A Note on the Feverel Crest." *Victorian Newsletter*, No. 26 (1964), p. 32.

Lees, F. N. "George Meredith, Novelist." *Pelican Guide* [1454], VI (1958), 324-337.

Lindsay, Jack. *George Meredith, His Life and Work*. London: The Bodley Head, 1956. [A suggestive interpretation, but strongly colored by political bias.]

McCormick, John. **Catastrophe** *and Imagination*. London: Longmans, Green, 1957.

Marshall, William H. "Richard Feverel: 'The Original Man.'" *Victorian Newsletter*, No. 18 (1960), 15-18.

Mayo, Robert D. "*The Egoist* and The Willow Pattern." *ELH*, IX (1940), 71-78.

Meredith, William Maxse. *The Letters of George Meredith*. New York: Charles Scribner's Sons, 1912.

Moffatt, James. *George Meredith: Introduction to His Novels.* New York and London: Hodder and Stoughton, 1909.

Morris, John W. "Inherent Principles of Order in Richard Feverel." *PMLA,* LXXVIII (1963), 333–340.

Peel, Robert, *The Creed of a Victorian Pagan.* Cambridge: Harvard University Press, 1931.

Petter, Guy B. *George Meredith and His German Critics.* London: H. F. and G. Witherby, 1939. [Good introduction to Meredith. Emphasizes his schooldays in Germany.]

Photiades, Constantin. *George Meredith: Sa Vie, Son Imagination, Son Art, Son Doctrine.* Paris: Libraire Armand Colin, 1910. [Translation by Arthur Price, New York: Charles Scribner's Sons, 1931.]

Priestley, J. B. *George Meredith.* "English Men of Letters Series." London: Macmillan, 1926.

Robinson, E. A. "Meredith's Literary Theory and Science." *PMLA,* LIII (1938).

Sassoon, Siegfried. *Meredith.* London: Constable, 1948.

Sencourt, Robert Esmond. *The Life of George Meredith.* New York: Charles Scribner's Sons, 1929.

Stevenson, Lionel. *Darwin Among the Poets.* Chicago: University of Chicago Press, 1932. [pp. 183–236 on Meredith. Valuable.]

_____."George Meredith." *Victorian Newsletter,* No. 13 (1958), 24. [Guide to Research Materials.]

_____."Meredith and the Problem of Style in the Novel." *Zeitschrift fur Anglistik und Amerikanistik* (East Berlin), VI (1958), 181-189.

_____."Meredith and the Problem of Style in the Novel." *Stil-und Formprobleme*, No. 5 (1960), 339-343.

_____.*The Ordeal of George Meredith.* New York: Charles Scribner's Sons, 1953. [Very useful recent critical biography.]

Swann, George Rogers. *Philosophical Parallelisms in Six English Novelists: The Conception of Good, Evil, and Human Nature.* "Pamphlets on the History of English Literature, VI." Philadelphia: University of Pennsylvania, 1920.

Talon, Henri A. "Le Comique, le Tragique, et la Romanesque dans *The Ordeal of Richard Feverel.*" *Etudes Anglaises*, XVII (1964), 241-261.

Thompson, Lawrence R. *A Comic Principle in Sterne, Meredith, and Joyce.* Oslo: University of Oslo, 1954.

Trevelyan, G. M. *The Poetry and Philosophy of George Meredith.* London: Constable, 1906.

Willey, Basil. *Nineteenth-Century Studies: Coleridge to Matthew Arnold.* London: Chatto & Windus, 1949. [Contains some material useful in interpreting Meredith.]

Wright, Walter F. *Art and Substance in George Meredith: A Study in Narrative.* Lincoln, Neb.: University of Nebraska Press, 1963. Bison Book, BB140. [Orig. pub. 1953.]

Zipf, G. K. *New Facts in the Early Life of George Meredith.* Harvard Studies in English, XX (1938).

THE POETRY OF GEORGE MEREDITH

See Maurice Buxton Forman, *A Bibliography of the Writings in Prose and Verse of George Meredith* (Edinburgh: Printed for the Bibliographical Society at the Dunedin Press, 1922) for description of the editions and information concerning publication.

Poems, 1851

Modern Love and Poems of the English Roadside, With Poems and Ballads, 1862.

Poems and Lyrics of the Joy of Earth, 1883.

***Ballads** and Poems of Tragic Life*, 1887.

A Reading of Earth, 1888.

Jump-to-Glory Jane, 1889.

Modern Love, A Reprint: To Which is added The Sage Enamoured and the Honest Lady, 1892.

Poems: The Empty Purse, with Odes to the Comic Spirit, To Youth in Memory, and Verses, 1892.

Odes in Contribution to the Song of French History, 1898. Poems, Vol. 111, 1898.

A Reading of Life, with other Poems, 1901.

Twenty Poems, 1909.

Last Poems, 1909.

Many of the poems in these volumes were first printed in periodicals; *The Thrush in* February first appeared in *Macmillan's Magazine*, Aug. 1885, pp. 265-271, and was included as part of *A Reading of Earth* in 1888.

Poems [Vol. XXIV, XXV, XXVI of the Memorial Edition of the Works of George Meredith]. Edinburgh: T. and A. Constable, 1909-11.

The Poetical Works of George Meredith, ed. with notes by G. M. Trevelyan. London: Constable and Co., Ltd., 1919; first publ. 1912; reprinted by Charles Scribner's Sons, N. Y., 1930. [The notes, although not extensive, are helpful. One important feature of this edition is that it includes the original date of publication of each poem.]

SELECTED CRITICAL WORKS DEALING AT SOME LENGTH WITH MEREDITH'S POETRY

Baker, Ernest A., *The History of the English Novel* (New York: Barnes and Noble, 1950), Vol. VIII. See especially Ch. vii, pp. 274-317, for discussion of Meredith's poetry and philosophy.

Beach, Joseph Warren, *The Concept of Nature in 19th-Century English Poetry* (N.Y.: Macmillan, 1936), ch. XVIII, pp. 470-99.

Hudson, Richard B. "The Meaning of Egoism in George Meredith's *The Egoist*," in *19th-Century Fiction*, vol. 3, no. 3, Dec. 1948, pp. 163-76.

Robinson, E. Arthur, "Meredith's Literary Theory and Science: Realism Versus the Comic Spirit" in *PMLA*, vol. LIII, no. 3, Sept. 1938, pp. 857-69.

Stevenson, Lionel, *Darwin Among the Poets* (Chicago: Univ. of Chicago Press, 1932), ch. IV, pp. 183-236.

Trevelyan, G. M. *The Poetry and Philosophy of George Meredith*: (London: A. Constable and Co., 1906).

Wright, Walter F., *Art and Substance in George Meredith: A Study in Narrative* (Lincoln, Nebraska: Univ. of Nebraska Press, 1953).

SUGGESTIONS FOR FURTHER STUDY

The following possible topics for research are suggestive, not exhaustive; some of them have been at least hinted at by the essays above on Meredith's philosophy and poetry:

1. Zoroastrianism and "the Magian Conflict" in Meredith.
2. Meredith's **satire** of "scientific humanism."
3. The meanings of sentimentalism, egoism, asceticism, and sensualism in a Meredithian context.
4. The relation of Meredith's poetry to his fiction; Meredith as poet; philosophical poetry.
5. The Vitalism of *Diana of the Crossways*; *The Egoist*; *The Ordeal of Richard Feverel*.
6. The use of the poetic novel.
7. Autobiographical elements in Meredith's fiction.
8. Dramatic technique in *The Ordeal of Richard Feverel*.
9. The meaning of *Modern Love*.
10. Blood, Brain, and Spirit-the Meredithian ethical triad.
11. The fictional tradition of Thomas Love Peacock as reflected in Meredith's writings.
12. The function of Comedy; the relation of Meredith's Essay on Comedy to his novels.
13. *Evan Harrington* as an autobiographical novel.
14. Shakespearean elements in *The Ordeal of Richard Feverel*.
15. Meredith as a writer of tragedy.
16. Meredith's philosophy and theory of Art as revealed in his letters.

17. Uncollected manuscripts of Meredith's fiction.
18. A critical history of *The Ordeal of Richard Feverel* from its publication to the present.
19. The tradition of courtesy-literature in Meredith's fiction.
20. Meredith's philosophical vocabulary and its sources in science and education.

www.ingramcontent.com/pod-product-compliance
Lightning Source LLC
LaVergne TN
LVHW021708060526
838200LV00050B/2565